THE CAMPAIGN

OF

CHANCELLORSVILLE

BY

THEODORE A. DODGE

NEW INTRODUCTION

BY

STEPHEN W. SEARS

SECOND EDITION

DA CAPO PRESS • NEW YORK

Library of Congress Cataloging-in-Publication Data

Dodge, Theodore Ayrault, 1842–1909.
  The campaign of Chancellorsville / by Theodore A. Dodge.—1st Da
Capo Press ed.
    p.   cm.
  Originally published: Boston: Ticknor, 1881.
  ISBN 0-306-80914-1 (alk. paper)
  1. Chancellorsville (Va.), Battle of, 1863. I. Title.
E475.35.D64   1999
973.7'33—dc21   98-54968
                                                                       CIP

First Da Capo Press edition 1999

This Da Capo Press paperback edition of *The Campaign of
Chancellorsville* is an unabridged republication of the second edition
published in Boston in 1886, with the deletion of four fold-out maps
and the addition of a new introduction by Stephen W. Sears.

New introduction copyright © 1999 by Stephen W. Sears

Published by Da Capo Press, Inc.
A Member of Perseus Books Group
233 Spring Street, New York, N.Y. 10013

Manufactured in the United States of America

INTRODUCTION

Chancellorsville presented a particular challenge to nineteenth-century historians of the Civil War, especially those historians who wrote with a Northern slant—which was most of them. Chancellorsville was, first of all, an enormously complex ten-day campaign (April 27–May 6, 1863), with intricate maneuvering and convoluted high-command decisions that defied easy analysis. And, secondly, it was a Union defeat—an unexpectedly resounding defeat—that did not make for very pleasant reading. The North, it was generally agreed, *should* have won that battle; the challenge was to explain why it had not.

It is not surprising, then, that the first full history of the Battle of Chancellorsville would come from Southern pens. In 1867 Colonel William Allan, the self-appointed historian of the Army of Northern Virginia, and Major Jed Hotchkiss, the very able cartographer of that army, collaborated on a book titled *The Battle-Fields of Vir-*

ginia: Chancellorsville. This was intended as the first in a series of volumes recording the major battles of the Army of Northern Virginia, but, as Douglas Southall Freeman observed, "the times were not propitious for historical work of the quality the two men were determined to do." The Hotchkiss-Allan *Chancellorsville* proved to be the only fruit of this collaboration. The challenge of understanding and explaining such battles as Chancellorsville was then taken up by the Military Historical Society of Massachusetts.

The Society was founded in Boston in 1876. "Its chief object," announced the founders, "is the investigation of questions relating to the late War of the Rebellion." Committees were appointed from the membership to investigate "given questions"—especially the more difficult questions—and papers were delivered, discussed, criticized, and published periodically in the volumes of the Society's *Papers*. Over the course of time, Lieutenant Colonel Theodore Ayrault Dodge, among all the Society's members, was acknowledged to be the expert on Chancellorsville.

Theodore Dodge was Massachusetts-born, in 1842, and was raised in Pittsfield, an intellectually flavored haven in the Berkshires for the literary elite of the time. Among the residents of the Pittsfield area were Oliver Wendell Holmes and Herman Melville. Perhaps there was a telling influence here, for Dodge proved to be one of the more articulate soldiers of his generation. According to a later sketch of him that appeared in the *Boston Herald*, in his teens Dodge spent some time in Berlin, "where he received his military education under General von

Froneich, of the Prussian army." Presumably this was a military school; what is certain is that he was in Berlin long enough to learn to speak German fluently. Dodge would find use for this language skill during his Civil War career.

The news of Fort Sumter brought Dodge home from Europe, and, at age nineteen, he volunteered in the Northern cause. He enlisted in the 101st New York, one of that state's numerous two-year regiments. Its first recruits were mustered in September 1861, but it was not until March 1862 that the 101st left New York for the seat of war. After service in the Washington defenses, the regiment was sent to the Peninsula to reinforce Philip Kearny's division of the Third Corps. The regiment experienced its baptism of fire at Oak Grove, the first of the Seven Days' Battles, where, in common with most new regiments, it was rather roughly handled. The 101st then saw some action at Glendale and Malvern Hill, and ended the Seven Days with a casualty list of 44, half of whom were missing or taken prisoner.

In his letters home from the Peninsula (preserved today in the Manuscript Division, Library of Congress), Theodore Dodge revealed a sharp and highly observant eye. He described the balloonist "Professor" Thaddeus Lowe, for example, as "a 'big-wig'—rank of Colonel—pay ditto—shoulder straps of bullion with a balloon on these in rich silver—swell trains carrying inflators—100 men at his disposal. . . . Fine cloth coats and little boots (so as to not weigh down the balloon. I suppose), handsome horses, wall tents, and commander in chief of the Balloon

Department of the Army of the Potomac!! Fine high position whether up or down, is it not?"

By the time of Second Bull Run, Dodge had been promoted first lieutenant and was named regimental adjutant. The now-veteran 101st New York was heavily engaged in that battle, losing 124 men and gaining hard-to-please Phil Kearny's praise for its "high character." Adjutant Dodge, wrote the regimental commander in his after-action report, "was of great service to me." This would prove to be Dodge's last service to the 101st, however. The regiment was greatly understrength—it engaged only 153 enlisted men at Second Bull Run; by year's end it would disappear from the army's rolls in a consolidation with the 37th New York. Well before that time, recognizing the slim future prospects for an officer where he was, Dodge resigned and found himself a new berth—still as first lieutenant and regimental adjutant—with the newly recruited 119th New York volunteers.

The 119th is described in Ella Lonn's *Foreigners in the Union Army and Navy* as one of New York's several "half-German regiments." (The state fielded ten "solidly German" regiments.) Raised in New York City and mustered in on September 4, 1862, the 119th was promptly dispatched to Washington and assigned to Carl Schurz's division of the Eleventh Corps. It was this corps assignment, probably more than anything else, that in later years would inspire Dodge to devote so much of his historian's attention to the Battle of Chancellorsville. The Eleventh Corps became infamous—at least so far as the rest of the Army of the Potomac was concerned—as the scapegoat for the Chancellorsville defeat. That, understandably, did not sit well with Theodore Ayrault Dodge.

"I must say," adjutant Dodge wrote home on November 21, 1862, "the 119th is not as easy a Regiment to manage as was the 101st. There are Germans who dont understand English, Frenchmen ditto, Swedes and Spaniards who dont understand anything, and Italians who are worse than all the rest together." The 119th's regimental commander, too, was someone out of the ordinary. Colonel Elias Peissner bore a striking resemblance to King Ludwig I of Bavaria, or so wrote divisional commander Schurz in his memoirs—striking, according to Schurz, because he was in fact the natural son of that famously amorous and eccentric monarch. Colonel Peissner, who in peacetime had been a professor at Union College in upstate New York, was thus colorful enough in reputation to be right at home as head of this colorfully polyglot regiment. By background, too, Lieutenant Dodge found himself at home in the half-German 119th regiment in the largely German Eleventh Corps.

The men of the Eleventh Corps, since their enlistment and up until February 1863, served pridefully under the command of Franz Sigel. "I fights mit Sigel" was their boast. Dodge described the corps commander as "a little man, not more than 5 ft. 5 and was anything but military in his appearance this morning. He was dressed in a nondescript coat, several sizes too large for him, lined with fur . . . ; his feet were encased in shoes also lined with fur and several sizes too large for him. . . . In the corner were a pair of boots which looked large enough for the general to hide in. . . . He has not good features except his eye, which is sharp and expressive. I should judge that he spoke English with only tolerable facility, but in this I may be mistaken, as our conversation was entirely in German. . . . It seems very curious to speak German to everybody here. It is like a German settlement. In fact when I see a soldier I involuntarily speak German to him." The bilingual Dodge must have been one of the more treasured staff adjutants in the Army of the Potomac.

Even at the tender age of twenty, Dodge revealed a bent for military analysis. In December 1862, commenting on Burnside's disastrous Fredericksburg campaign, he asked his homefolks, "Why is it we are always defeated? I cannot understand it, for the rebels *do not* fight better than we do. They are *certainly better led* & have I believe more heart in the cause. But we ought certainly to beat them by force of numbers. It is curious, however, with 500,000 men they should always at given points oppose to us superior numbers, while we have 1,000,000 men. All this is strategy."

In his later Civil War writings, and notably in regard to Chancellorsville, Dodge would devote much effort and many pages to appraising the Union high command. He formed definite views on that topic right from the first. The command upheaval he witnessed in the Army of the Potomac over the winter of 1862–'63—beginning with the removal of George B. McClellan and ending with the appointment of Joseph Hooker—offered food for his thought.

"I believe, in fact I know justly," Dodge wrote on January 28, 1863, two days after Hooker's appointment, "he is called Fighting Joe Hooker, but is he capable of handling 150,000 men? I fear not, any more than Burnside. Sumner & Franklin, who each commanded one of the Grand Divisions, and good generals they are too, have also been relieved, to McClellan influence out of the army, I guess. What ill or good it will do, is more than anyone can predict, but when a man is hauling a heavy load uphill, he has no time to stop and swap jackasses, . . . and if he have a team of six jackasses, it is still less advisable to stop and swap single ones, in my humble opinion."

His dubious initial opinion of Joe Hooker was not enhanced by a command change that general soon inflicted on Dodge's corps, the Eleventh. In place of Franz Sigel (a notable figure in the aborted revolution of 1848 in the German States and therefore much admired by the many first- and second-generation Germans in the corps), Hooker installed Oliver Otis Howard, a mediocre, colorless general whose one abiding interest was religious orthodoxy. The men of the Eleventh Corps, largely freethinkers, called Howard "Old Prayer Book" and entered upon the spring 1863 campaign with little confidence in his leadership.

Chancellorsville proved to be disastrous for Howard and the Eleventh Corps in general, and for Dodge's 119th New York in particular. At first, in the opening days of the campaign, Dodge (in common with most of his fellow soldiers) was delighted with Hooker's leadership. "Bravo for Hooker!" Dodge wrote exuberantly in a May 1 letter. "So far this movement has been beautifully planned and executed." One day later, however, Stonewall Jackson's celebrated flank attack surprised and routed Howard's Eleventh Corps. The 119th's commander, Colonel Peissner, was killed in the opening moments of the assault, and the regiment fled the field with a loss of 120 men. The Eleventh Corps suffered some 2,400 casualties that day, over forty per cent of them taken prisoner.

"Oh! that our Corps had stood its ground," Dodge wrote disconsolently to his family on May 12, after the army had retreated back across the Rappahannock to its old camps. "I am ashamed that even any number of the enemy should have been able to drive us from our position. To be sure we were the Right Flank of the army, and when outflanked we were the first to suffer. But is any explanation enough to justify our being so badly beaten?" Dodge's search for an explanation would continue for better than two decades.

His service in the field, however, did not last beyond the Army of the Potomac's next battle. At Gettysburg on the first day, July 1 (when Rebels again roughly treated the Eleventh Corps), Dodge was severely wounded, losing his right leg below the knee to amputation. He was one of 140 casualties in his regiment.

Upon his recuperation, Dodge elected to remain in the service, in the Veteran Reserve Corps, and was promoted captain. His administrative skills so impressed the War Department that in May 1864, at the age of only 22, he was put in charge of the Enrollment Branch, to manage the record-keeping for "citizens subject to military duty." In December 1864, now Major Dodge, he shifted to head the Deserters' Branch, with the task of arresting wartime deserters. Dodge remained in the army after the war, much of the time in the War Department. When he finally retired from service in 1870, as a brevet lieutenant colonel, he was all of 28 years old.

Beginning a second, civilian career, Dodge studied law and became, so a biographical sketch explained, "a successful industrialist." Before he was forty, he had so managed his new career that he had the leisure to devote considerable time to his avocation, military history—most especially, Civil War military history.

Dodge's first writing on the war was an article in *Galaxy* in 1868, when he was still in the army, titled "Tied Up by the Thumbs," on the subject of military discipline in the late war. The next year, still in service, he wrote "Left Wounded on the Field" for *Putnam's*. He drew this article from his experiences at Gettysburg, describing in personal terms what combat was like, and how it felt to be wounded on that bloody field.

He seems to have more sharply focused his military history interests after becoming a charter member of the Military Historical Society of Massachusetts in 1876. That focus, with the encouragement of the Society, was on Chancellorsville. In 1880 and 1881, Dodge prepared and delivered to the membership three papers on that campaign.

The first paper, not surprisingly, dealt with the phase of the battle with which Dodge was most familiar—"The

Disaster of the 11th Corps at Chancellorsville." This article detailed Jackson's flank attack on Howard's corps on May 2, which Dodge had witnessed firsthand as adjutant of the 119th New York. His second paper dealt with "The Fight on Sunday, May 3, 1863." Here, at and around Chancellorsville, was the decisive action of the ten-day campaign, and the fiercest and costliest fighting as well for both sides. Dodge titled his third paper "General Sedgwick's Operations in the Chancellorsville Campaign." This described John Sedgwick's complex movements during the campaign, on the Fredericksburg front, while in command of the Federal left wing. These, in Dodge's view, represented the three crucial phases of the Chancellorsville campaign—an opinion that is still valid.

The next year, 1881, Dodge published the first edition of *The Campaign of Chancellorsville*. The publisher was James R. Osgood of Boston. The three papers Dodge delivered to the Military Historical Society of Massachusetts made up the core of the book. Dodge's was the second full history of Chancellorsville—after the Hotchkiss-Allan volume—and the first to be written by a Northern participant.

What sets Dodge's work apart from what had preceded it—in particular Hotchkiss-Allan (1867), and the chapter on the battle in William Swinton's general history of the war (1866)—is his use of sources. The volumes of the *Official Records of the Union and Confederate Armies* covering Chancellorsville would not appear until 1889, but a partial, preliminary, very limited edition, a sort of demi-*Official Records*, was in the process of being compiled in the 1870s. Through Dodge's connections in the War Department (fortified during his 1864–'70 army service), and using the good offices of the Military Historical Society of Massachusetts (Robert N. Scott, head of the War Records Office, was a corresponding member of the Society), he gained first-time access to official reports and correspondence relating to the campaign and battle. Although Dodge's is primarily a Unionist account, he used these same connections to gain access to appropriate Confederate records. Consequently, this volume is the first truly authoritative study of the Battle of Chancellorsville.

Indeed, *The Campaign of Chancellorsville* would remain the authoritative study for almost three decades and throughout its author's lifetime. Dodge died in 1909. Only in 1910, when John Bigelow's massive (and massively detailed) study of Chancellorsville was published, did a new standard work appear.

It was by means of a second and revised edition of *The Campaign of Chancellorsville*—here reprinted—that Dodge maintained his historian's edge in regard to this battle. For the second edition his publisher was Ticknor & Company, also of Boston, and although Ticknor retained the original first-edition publishing date of 1881, the actual date of publication was 1886. This is an important point, for it assures us that Theodore Dodge had examined and appraised the small rush of publications covering Chancellorsville that appeared shortly after his first edition was published.

Abner Doubleday's *Chancellorsville and Gettysburg* (also available from Da Capo Press), in Scribner's "Campaigns of the Civil War" series, was published in 1882. General Doubleday's coverage of Chancellorsville is comparatively brief, and because Doubleday was posted far from the center of the fighting on that field, there is (unlike Dodge) little of a participant's flavor to his account. Samuel P. Bates's *The Battle of Chancellorsville*, also published in 1882, had the blessing of General Hooker himself, who critiqued its contents beforehand and provided Bates with certain documents. But except for several unique episodes courtesy of Joe Hooker, Bates produced a pedestrian, poorly written work. Dodge also acknowledged seeing the chapter on Chancellorsville in the American edition (1883) of the Comte de Paris's *History of the Civil War in America*, as well as articles on the campaign in *The Century* magazine's "Battles and Leaders of the Civil War" series.

Except for deflating the Chancellorsville role of Union cavalryman Alfred Pleasonton (a shameless self-promoter), Dodge did not feel obliged to undertake a wholesale make-over for his second edition. He explained his reasoning in a paper delivered to the Military Historical Society of Massachusetts in 1886. "The demand for a new edition now enables me to correct this mistake in my book," he told his audience in regard to the Pleasonton case. "This error is, however, the only one which, in the light of all which has been written since, I feel that I am honestly called upon to correct. I think that my criticisms upon Chancellorsville are fair and judicious, and the facts are undoubtedly stated with exactness." Theodore Dodge was no shrinking violet when it came to stating his case before the bar of history.

And in fact there is nothing at all tentative in *The Campaign of Chancellorsville*. It is a straightforward account by someone who was there, who has definite positive (and negative) views, and who is not hesitant to express them. In recounting the heat of the fighting Dodge is likely to switch to the present tense, a nineteenth-century historians' device that can be effective but takes some getting used to. Although the Confederates are certainly given their due here, this is a battle seen from a Northern perspective (just as the Hotchkiss-Allan work displays a Southern perspective). Theodore Dodge was out to explain why the Federals lost at Chancellorsville, not why the Rebels won.

"Colonel Dodge has given us a most excellent book," wrote Colonel William Allan in the *Southern Historical Society Papers*. "Amidst the mass of rubbish yearly printed about the war, it is refreshing to find an author more anxious to get at the truth than to glorify comrades, or vilify his foes; an author with the honesty, intelligence and patience to pick out the facts from the confused and often conflicting testimony, and the ability to state them clearly and fairly." Allan could be a very tough audience for Northern-written histories of the war, and no doubt Dodge was appreciative of the respect shown him from that quarter.

If Dodge may be thus justly praised for his honesty and fairness, it must also be pointed out (as William Allan remarked) that "One is struck throughout by the severity of Colonel Dodge's criticism of General Hooker." Indeed, wrote Allan, "the whole book is an arraignment of that officer's mode of conducting operations, and at times too much space is given to discussing the exact measure of responsibility which attached to him for various failures." While, as the commanding general, Hooker ultimately bore responsibility for the Chancellorsville defeat, Dodge portrays him here as responsible as well for each and every facet of that defeat.

In truth, the failings of Hooker's lieutenants—especially Generals Sedgwick and Howard and the commander of the Union cavalry, General Stoneman—were egregious in this campaign. The precise documentation of their failings was not known or available to Dodge when he was writing; but at least in the case of General Howard there is another factor at work here. The rout of Howard's Eleventh Corps, in which Dodge served so faithfully, was promptly branded by the rest of the army as the cause of the Chancellorsville defeat, and Dodge not unnaturally set out to correct that impression. It is ironic that, considering the disaster inflicted upon the Eleventh Corps, which eyewitness Dodge depicts here with such authority, he lets Howard off with far less censure than that general deserves.

Theodore Dodge continued writing and lecturing on the Civil War into the 1890s, and his *A Bird's-Eye View of Our Civil War* (1883) is one of the better early general histories of the conflict. But Dodge first made his mark as a Civil War historian with his narrative of the epic

Chancellorsville struggle. "This book is a valuable contribution to history," William Allan said of it, and that is a verdict as accurate today as when it was rendered.

STEPHEN W. SEARS
Norwalk, Connecticut
July 1998

STEPHEN W. SEARS is the editor of *The Civil War Papers of George B. McClellan* and author of *George B. McClellan: The Young Napoleon* (both available from Da Capo Press), as well as *Landscape Turned Red: The Battle of Antietam*, *To the Gates of Richmond: The Peninsula Campaign*, *Chancellorsville*, and, most recently, *Controversies and Commanders: Dispatches from the Army of the Potomac*. He lives in Connecticut.

TO THE MEMBERS OF

THE MILITARY HISTORICAL SOCIETY

OF MASSACHUSETTS,

OF WHOSE RESEARCHES INTO THE HISTORY OF OUR CIVIL
WAR THE FOLLOWING PAGES FORM BUT
A MODEST PART,

This Volume is, with Sincere Regard, Dedicated

BY THE AUTHOR.

CONTENTS.

THE

CAMPAIGN OF CHANCELLORSVILLE.

I.

INTRODUCTION.

IT must seem to the casual reader of the history of
the war of 1861–65, that enough has already been
written upon the campaign of Chancellorsville. And there
are numerous brilliant essays, in the histories now before
the public, which give a *coup-d'œil* more or less accurate
of this ten-days' passage of arms. But none of these
spread before the reader facts sufficiently detailed to illustrate the particular theory advanced by each to account
for the defeat of the Army of the Potomac on this field.

The stigma besmirching the character of the Eleventh
Corps, and of Howard, its then commanding general, for a
panic and rout in but a small degree owing to them; the
unjust strictures passed upon Sedgwick for his failure to
execute a practically impossible order; the truly remarkable blunders into which Gen. Hooker allowed himself to
lapse, in endeavoring to explain away his responsibility for
the disaster; the bare fact, indeed, that the Army of the
Potomac was here beaten by Lee, with one-half its force;

1

and the very partial publication, thus far, of the details of the campaign, and the causes of our defeat, — may stand as excuse for one more attempt to make plain its operations to the survivors of the one hundred and eighty thousand men who there bore arms, and to the few who harbor some interest in the subject as mere history.

To say that Gen. Hooker lapsed into blunders in explaining his share in this defeat, is to use a form of words purposely tempered to the memory of a gallant soldier, who, whatever his shortcomings, has done his country signal service; and to avoid the imputation of baldly throwing down the gauntlet of ungracious criticism. All reference to Gen. Hooker's skill or conduct in this, one of the best conceived and most fatally mismanaged of the many unsuccessful advances of the Army of the Potomac, is made with sincere appreciation of his many admirable qualities, frankly, and untinged by bitterness. But it must be remembered, that Gen. Hooker has left himself on record as the author of many harsh reflections upon his subordinates; and that to mete out even justice to all requires unvarnished truth.

The most uncalled-for slur upon the conduct of his lieutenants probably occurs in his testimony before the Committee on the Conduct of the War. Before withdrawing from the south side of the Rappahannock, after the decisive events of the battle-field had cooped up the army between the river and its intrenchments, Hooker called together all his corps commanders, and requested their several opinions as to the advisability of attack or retreat. Whatever discussion may have then been had, it was generally understood, in after-days, that all but one of these generals had expressed himself freely for an immediate advance. In referring to this understanding, while denying its correctness, Hooker used the following language : —

"So far as my experience extends, there are in all armies officers more valiant after the fight than while it is pending; and, when a truthful history of the Rebellion shall be written, it will be found that the Army of the Potomac is not an exception."

Merely to characterize as ungenerous this aspersion upon the courage of such men as then served under Hooker, savors of error on the side of leniency. And, inasmuch as these words strike, as it were, the keynote of all the statements which Hooker has vouchsafed with reference to these events, they might be assumed fairly to open the door to unsparing criticism. But it is hoped that this course has been avoided ; and that what censure is dealt out to Gen. Hooker in the succeeding pages will be accepted, even by his advocates, in the kindly spirit in which it is meant, and in which every soldier of the beloved old Army of the Potomac must uniformly refer to every other.

There is, moreover, no work on Chancellorsville which results from research into all records now accessible.

The work of Allan and Hotchkiss, of 1867, than which nothing can be more even-handed, or more admirable as far as it goes, adopts generally the statements made in the reports of the Confederate generals : and these are necessarily one-sided ; reports of general officers concerning their own operations invariably are.   Allan and Hotchkiss wrote with only the Richmond records before them, in addition to such information from the Federal standpoint as may be found in general orders, the evidence given before the Committee on the Conduct of the War, and newspaper correspondence.   At that time many of the Federal reports were not to be had: such as were at the War Department were hardly accessible.   Reports had been duly made by all superior officers engaged in and surviving this campaign, excepting only the general in command; but, strange to say, not only did Gen. Hooker refrain from making a report, but he retained in his personal possession many of the records of the Army of the Potomac covering the period of his command, and it is only since his death that these records have been in part recovered by the Secretary of War.   Some are still missing, but they probably contain no important matter not fully given elsewhere.

Although Hooker testified before the Committee on the Conduct of the War: "Without an exception I forwarded to that office " — the War Department — "all the reports and returns and information concerning the army, and furnished them promptly, and, as I think, as no other army commander has done," his memory had at the moment played him traitor, for a considerable part of these records were not disposed of as stated.   It should be remarked, however, that Hooker is not singular in this leaning towards the *meum* in the matter of records.

The sources relied on for the facts herein given are the reports of the officers engaged, both Federal and Confederate, added to many private notes, memoranda, and maps, made by them ; the testimony before the Committee on the Conduct of the War, which included Hooker's examination ; and the maps made by the Engineer Department of the United-States Army, and those of Capt. Hotchkiss.

This latter officer was the topographical engineer of the Second Corps of the Army of Northern Virginia, and made his surveys by order of Gen. Lee immediately after the campaign. They are of the greatest assistance and value.

Eighteen years have elapsed since North and South crossed swords upon this memorable field; and it would seem that all Americans can now contemplate with unruffled heart the errors under which " the Army of the Potomac was here beaten without ever being fought," as well as boast with equal pride, not only of the abundant courage displayed by either side, but of the calm skill with which Gen. Lee wrested victory from a situation desperately compromised, and of the genius of that greatest of his lieutenants, Thomas J. Jackson, who here sealed with his blood his fidelity to the cause he loved so well.

It has been said that this campaign furnishes as much material for the psychological as for the military student. And certainly nothing less than a careful analysis of Hooker's character can explain the abnormal condition into which his mental and physical energy sank during the second act of this drama. He began with really masterly moves, speedily placing his wary adversary at the saddest disadvantage. But, having attained this height, his power seemed to pass away as from an overtasked mind. With twice the weight of arm, and as keen a blade, he appeared quite unable to parry a single lunge of Lee's, quite unable to thrust himself. He allowed his corps commanders to be beaten in detail, with no apparent effort to aid them from his abundant resources, the while his opponent was demanding from every man in his command the last ounce of his strength. And he finally retired, dazed and weary, across the river he had so ably and boastingly placed behind him ten days before, against the opinion of nearly all his subordinates; for in this case the conditions were so plain that even an informal council of war advised a fight.

With character-study, however, this sketch has nothing to do. It is confined to describing events, and suggesting queries for the curious in military history.

II.

CONDITION OF THE COMBATANTS.

THE first two years of civil strife had closed. The American people, which so far had shown more aptness at learning than skill in waging war, may be said to have passed through its apprenticeship in arms. The broad plan of operations, intelligently but rudely conceived at the outset by the greater spirits among our commanders, began to be more clearly grasped. The political strategy of both contestants made Virginia the field on which the left wing of the Federal armies pivoted, while the right swung farther and farther south and east, and the Confederates gallantly struggled for every foot of territory, yielding only to the inexorable. This right wing had already possession of the Mississippi as far south as Vicksburg, around which place Grant was preparing to tighten his coils; it had occupied the line of the Tennessee River, and had rendered useless to the Confederates the railroad from Memphis to Chattanooga, which had been the great central artery between Richmond and the trans-Mississippi States. The Southern partisans, with Morgan and Forrest as typical chiefs, had up to this period played, in the West especially, a very important part. They as much exceeded our cavalry in enterprise as they had advantage over it in knowledge of the country and in assistance from its population. They had on more than one occasion tapped the too long and slender lines of operation of our foremost armies. They had sent Grant to the right-about from his first march on Vicksburg, thus neutralizing Sherman's attempt at Chickasaw Bayou. They had compelled Buell to forfeit his hardly-earned footing, and to fall back from the Tennessee River to Louisville at the double-quick in order to beat Bragg in the race towards the gate of the Northern States, which disaster was happily soon retrieved by the latter's bloody check before Murfreesborough. Yet, despite these back-sets, the general course of events showed that Providence remained on the side of the heaviest battalions; and the spring of 1863 saw our armies extended from the pivot midway between the rival capitals in a more or less irregular line, and interrupted by the Alleghany Mountains, to Vicksburg and the Father of Waters.

Great as was the importance of success in Virginia, the Confederates had appreciated the fact as had not the political soldiers at the head of the Federal department of war. Our resources always enabled us to keep more men, and more and better material, on this battle-ground, than the Confederates could do; but this strength was constantly offset by the ability of the Southern generals, and their independence of action, as opposed to the frequent unskilfulness of ours, who were not only never long in command, but were then tied hand and foot to some ideal plan for insuring the safety of Washington. The political conditions under which the Army of the Poto-mac had so far constantly acted had never allowed it to do justice to its numbers, mobility, or courage ; while Mr. Lincoln, who actually assumed the powers of commander-in-chief, technically intrusted to him by the Constitution, was swayed to and fro by his own fears for the safety of his capital, and by political schemes and military obtuse-ness at his elbow.

Whether the tedious delays and deferred success, occa-sioned by these circumstances, were not eventually a ben-efit, in that they enabled the country to bring forth in the fulness of time the conditions leading to the extinguish-ment of slavery, which an earlier close of the war might not have seen ; not to mention the better appreciation by either combatant of the value of the other, which a strug-gle to the bitter end alone could generate, — is a ques-tion for the political student. But it will always remain in doubt whether the practical exhaustion of the resources of the South was not a condition precedent to ending the war, — whether, in sooth, the "last ditch" was not actu-ally reached when Lee surrendered at Appomattox.

In the West, merit had by this time brought to the sur-face the generals who later led us to successful victories. Their distance from the central controlling power resulted in their being let alone to work out their own salvation. Opposed to them had been some excellent but not the best of the Confederate leaders ; while Virginia boasted the *élite* of the Southern troops, the strongest of the cap-tains, and the most daring of the lieutenants, developed by the war.

Since the Russian campaign of Bonaparte, no such vast forces had been under arms. To command these required not only the divine military spark, but hardly-acquired experience. And the mimic war which the elements of European army life always affords had been wanting to educate our generals. It is not wonderful, then, that two years of fruitless campaigning was needed to teach our leaders how to utilize on such difficult *terrain* material equally vast in extent and uncouth in quality. For, however apt the American to learn the trade of war, — or any other, — it is a moot-point whether his independence of character is compatible with the perfect soldier, as typified in Friedrich's regiments, or the Old Guard.

But ability, native or acquired, forced its way to the front; and the requisite experience was gradually gained, for the school was one where the trade was quickly taught. Said Gen. Meade on one occasion, "The art of war must be acquired like any other. Either an officer must learn it at the academy, or he must learn it by experience in the field. Provided he *has* learned it, I don't care whether he is a West-Pointer, or not."

In the East, then, the army had been led by McDowell, McClellan, Pope, and Burnside, to victory and defeat equally fruitless. The one experiment so far tried, of giving the Army of the Potomac a leader from the West, culminating in the disaster of the second Bull Run, was not apt to be repeated within the year. That soldier of equal merit and modesty, whom the Army of the Potomac had been gradually educating as its future and permanent leader, was still unpretentiously commanding a corps, and learning by the successes and failures of his superiors. And who shall say that the results accomplished by Grant, Sherman, Thomas, Sheridan, and Meade, were not largely due to their good fortune in not being too early thrust to the front? "For," as says Swinton, "it was inevitable that the first leaders should be sacrificed to the nation's ignorance of war."

In the South, the signs of exhaustion had not yet become grave. The conscription act, passed in April, 1862, had kept the ranks full. The hope of foreign intervention, though distant, was by no means wholly abandoned. Financial matters had not yet assumed an entirely desperate complexion. Nor had the belief in the royalty of cotton received its *coup de grâce*. The vigor and courage of the Confederacy were unabated, and the unity of parties in the one object of resistance to invasion doubled its effective strength. Perhaps this moment was the flood-tide of Southern enthusiasm and confidence; which, after the Pennsylvania campaign, began to ebb. It is not intended to convey the idea that the South was prosperous. On the contrary, those who read the signs aright, saw and predicted its approaching decline. But, as far as its power of resistance went, it was at its highest when compared with the momentarily lessened aggressiveness of the North. For the anti-war party was doing its best to tie the hands of the administration; and, while this in no wise lessened the flow of men and material to the front, it produced a grave effect upon the moral strength which our chiefs were able to infuse into their method of conducting the war.

III.

HOOKER AND THE ARMY OF THE POTOMAC.

THE unfortunate course of events during the early winter of 1862–63 had resulted in a grievous loss of *morale* in the Army of the Potomac. The useless slaughter of Marye's Heights was, after a few weeks, succeeded by that most huge of all strategic jokes, the Mud March; and Gen. Burnside retired from a position he had never sought, to the satisfaction, and, be it said to his credit, with the warm personal regard, of all. Sumner, whom the weight of years had robbed of strength, but not of gallantry, was relieved at his own request; Franklin was shelved. Hooker thus became senior general officer, and succeeded to the command.

No man enjoyed a more enviable reputation in the Army of the Potomac. He had forced himself upon its notice. From Bull Run, after which action he is said to have remarked to Mr. Lincoln that he knew more than any one on that field; through Williamsburg, where he so gallantly held his own against odds during the entire day, and with exhausted ammunition, until relieved by Kearney; before Richmond; during the Seven Days; in the railroad-cutting at Manassas; at Antietam, where he forced the fighting with so much determination, if not wisdom, on the Union right; up to Fredericksburg, where, after a personal protest to his commanding officer, he went in and fought his troops "until he thought he had lost as many men as he was ordered to lose," — Hooker's character as man and soldier had been marked. His commands so far had been limited; and he had a frank, manly way of winning the hearts of his soldiers. He was in constant motion about the army while it lay in camp; his appearance always attracted attention; and he was as well known to almost every regiment as its own commander. He was a representative man.

It is not astonishing that Mr. Lincoln, or the Washington pseudo-strategists who were his military advisers, could not distinguish, in selecting a chief who should be capable of leading the Army of the Potomac to victory, between the gallant corps-commander, who achieves brilliant results under limited responsibility, and the leader, upon whose sole resources of mind and courage devolve not only the instruction for health, equipment, rationing, march, or attack, of each of his subordinates, but the graver weight of prompt and correct decision and immediate action under every one of the kaleidoscopic changes of a campaign or a battle-field. It required more knowledge of the requisites of war, as well as a broader judgment of character, than Mr. Lincoln had had opportunity to form of the several soldiers of the army, to insure a happy choice.

And, doubtless, Hooker's self-assertiveness, success as a brigade, division, and corps commander, and decided appearance of large ability, shared equally in procuring his appointment. No one will deny Hooker's capacity in certain directions, or up to a given test. His whole career shows an exceptional power in "riding to orders." But he sadly lacked that rare combination of qualities and reserve power necessary to lead a hundred and twenty-five thousand men against such a foe as Lee.

Nothing shows more curiously a weak spot in Hooker's character than the odd pride he took in Mr. Lincoln's somewhat equivocal letter to him at the time of his appointment, here following: —

> EXECUTIVE MANSION, WASHINGTON, D.C.,
> Jan. 26, 1863.

MAJOR-GEN. HOOKER.

General, — I have placed you at the head of the Army of the Potomac. Of course, I have done this upon what appears to me to be sufficient reasons, and yet I think it best for you to know that there are some things in regard to which I am not quite satisfied with you. I believe you to be a brave and skilful soldier, which of course I like. I also believe you do not mix politics with your profession, in which you are right. You have confidence in yourself; which is a valuable, if not an indispensable, quality. You are ambitious, which, within reasonable bounds, does good rather than harm; but I think that during Gen. Burnside's command of the army, you have taken counsel of your ambition, and thwarted him as much as you could, in which you did a great wrong to the country and to a most meritorious and honorable brother-officer. I have heard, in such way as to believe it, of your recently saying that both the army and the Government needed a dictator. Of course, it was not for this, but in spite of it, that I have given you the command. Only those generals who gain success can set up dictators. What I now ask of you is military success, and I will risk the dictatorship. The Government will support you to the utmost of its ability, which is neither more nor less than it has done or will do for all commanders. I much fear that the spirit you have aided to infuse into the army, of criticising their commander and withholding confidence from him, will now turn upon you. I shall assist you as far as I can to put it down. Neither you nor Napoleon, if he were alive again, could get any good out of an army while such a spirit prevails in it. And now beware of rashness. Beware of rashness, but with energy and sleepless vigilance go forward, and give us victories.

Yours very truly,

A. LINCOLN.

Hooker was appointed Jan. 26, 1863; and Burnside, with a few earnest words, took leave of the army.

The troops received their new chief with a heartiness and confidence, which, since McClellan's re-instatement, had not been equalled. Hooker was to all the soul and embodiment of the growth and history of this weather-beaten Army of the Potomac. And the salutary changes he at once began to make, — for Hooker never lacked the power of organization, — were accepted with alacrity; and a spirit of cheerful willingness succeeded speedily to what had been almost a defiant obedience.

The army was in a lamentably low state of efficiency. Politics mingled with camp duties; and the disaffection of officers and men, coupled with an entire lack of confidence in the ability of the Army of the Potomac to accomplish any thing, were pronounced. Desertions occurred at the rate of two hundred a day, facilitated by relatives, who sent from home civilian clothing to soldiers at the front. Hooker states that he found 2,922 officers, and 81,964 enlisted men, entered as absent on the rolls of the army, a large proportion from causes unknown. Sharp and efficient measures were at once adopted, which speedily checked this alarming depletion of the ranks. Furloughs in reasonable quantity were allowed to deserving men and a limited number of officers. Work was found for the rank and file in drill and outpost duty sufficient to prevent idle habits. The commissariat was closely watched, and fresh rations more frequently issued, which much improved the health of the army. The system of picket-duty was more thoroughly developed, and so vigilantly carried out as to impress its importance upon, as well as teach its details to, the troops.

The cavalry, hitherto distributed by regiments throughout the army, was now consolidated into one corps, and from this time became a valuable element in the service, for it daily grew in efficiency. And such opportunities of doing field-work as a body were afforded it as circumstances allowed.

The grand divisions of Burnside were abolished, and the army divided into seven infantry corps.

The testimony of all general officers of the Army of the Potomac concurs in awarding the highest praise to Hooker for the manner in which he improved the condition of the troops during the three months he was in command prior to Chancellorsville. Himself says before the Committee on the Conduct of the War: " During the season of preparation the army made rapid strides in discipline, instruction and *morale*, and early in April was in a condition to inspire the highest expectations." And Swinton well sums up: "Under Hooker's influence the tone of the army underwent a change which would appear astonishing had not its elastic vitality been so often proved."

On the 30th of April the Army of the Potomac, exclusive of provost-guard, consisted of about a hundred and thirty thousand men under the colors, — "for duty equipped," according to the morning report, — distributed among the several army corps as follows: —

1st Corps, Gen. Reynolds . .	Wadsworth, Robinson, Doubleday,	16,908
2d Corps, Gen. Couch . .	Hancock, Gibbon, French,	16,893
3d Corps, Gen. Sickles . .	Birney, Berry, Whipple,	18,721
5th Corps, Gen. Meade . .	Griffin, Humphreys, Sykes,	15,724
6th Corps, Gen. Sedgwick . .	Brooks, Howe, Newton,	23,667
11th Corps, Gen. Howard .	Devens, Schurz, Steinwehr,	12,977
12th Corps, Gen. Slocum . .	Williams, Geary,	13,450
Cavalry Corps, Gen. Stoneman .	Pleasonton, Gregg, Averell, Buford, Reserve Brigade,	11,541
Artillery, Gen. Hunt, about 400 guns. Artillery reserve .		1,610
Total		131,491

IV.

THE ARMY OF NORTHERN VIRGINIA.

WHILE the Army of the Potomac lay about Falmouth, awaiting orders to move, Lee occupied the heights south of the Rappahannock, from Banks's Ford above, to Port Royal (or Skenker's Neck) below Fredericksburg, a line some fifteen miles in length as the crow flies. The crests of the hills on which lay the Army of Northern Virginia were from three-quarters of a mile to a mile and a half back from, and substantially parallel to, the river. Rifle-pits commanded every available crossing, which, being few and difficult, were easily guarded. Continuous lines of infantry parapets, broken by battery epaulements located for sweeping the wide approaches from the river, extended the whole distance; while abattis strengthened every place which the nature of the ground allowed an attacking column to pass.

The roads by which the various detachments of the army could intercommunicate for concentration upon any given point were numerous and well kept up, and were familiar to all commanding and staff officers.

Lee's forces numbered about sixty thousand men, for duty, distributed in the following organizations. As the brigades nearly equalled our divisions in size, they are given by name.

Part of Longstreet's 1st Corps	Anderson's division.	Mahone's brigade. / Posey's " / Wilcox's " / Perry's " / Wright's "	17,000
	McLaws' division.	Kershaw's " / Semmes's " / Wofford's " / Barksdale's "	
Jackson's 2d Corps.	A. P. Hill's division.	Heth's " / Pender's " / Archer's " / McGown's " / Lane's " / Thomas's "	11,000
	D. H. Hill's division.	Ramseur's " / Rodes's " / Dole's " / Iverson's " / Colquitt's "	9,000
	Trimble's division.	Colston's " / Jones's " / Nichols's " / Paxton's "	6,000
	Early's division.	Gordon's " / Hays's " / Smith's " / Hoke's "	7,400
Stuart's Cavalry division .	Fitz Hugh Lee's brigade . .		1,800
	W. H. F. Lee's " . .		900
Artillery, 170 pieces .	. . . .		5,000
Total .	. . . .		58,100

Hotchkiss and Allan state that there may have been three to five thousand more men in line at the time of Hooker's attack.

As will be noticed from the table, only part of Longstreet's corps was present. The main body had been sent, about Feb. 1, under command of its chief, to operate in the region between Petersburg and Suffolk, where our forces under Peck were making a demonstration. This detail reduced Lee's army by nearly one-quarter.

During the winter, Lee's forces had been distributed as follows: —

The old battle-ground of Dec. 13 was occupied by the First Corps; while Jackson with his Second Corps held Hamilton's Crossing, and extended his lines down to Port Royal. Stuart's cavalry division prolonged the left to Beverly Ford on the upper Rappahannock, and scoured the country as far as the Pamunkey region. Hampton's brigade of cavalry had been sent to the rear to recruit, and Fitz Lee's had taken its place at Culpeper, from which point it extended so as to touch Lee's left flank at Banks's Ford. The brigade of W. H. F. Lee was on the Confederate right. Stuart retained command of the entire force, but had his headquarters at Culpeper.

The supplies of the army were received by the Fredericksburg and Richmond Railroad from the capital, and from the depots on the Virginia Central. Lee had been assiduous in re-organizing his forces, in collecting an abundance of supplies, in checking desertions, and in procuring re-enforcements. And the vigor with which the conscription was pushed swelled his strength so materially that in three months Jackson's corps alone shows an increase from a force of twenty-five thousand up to thirty-three thousand men "for duty." The staff of the army was created a separate organization. The cavalry had already been successfully consolidated. And now the artillery was embodied in a special organization under Gen. Pendleton, and an engineer regiment put on foot.

The *morale* of the Army of Northern Virginia could not be finer. The forced retreat of McClellan from before Richmond; the driving of Pope from his vaunted positions in its front; the Maryland campaign with its deliberate withdrawal from an army of twice its strength; finally the bloody check to Burnside, — had furnished a succession of triumphs which would lend any troops self-confidence and high courage. But, in addition to all this, the average of the men of this army were older and more hardened soldiers than those of the Army of the Potomac. The early conscription acts of the Confederacy had made it difficult for men once inured to the steady bearing and rough life of the soldier, and to the hard fare of camp-life, to withdraw from the ranks.

In Hooker's testimony before the Committee on the Conduct of the War occurs this tribute to the Confederate infantry: " Our artillery had always been superior to that of the rebels, as was also our infantry, except in discipline; and that, for reasons not necessary to mention, never did equal Lee's army. With a rank and file vastly inferior to our own, intellectually and physically, that army has, by discipline alone, acquired a character for steadiness and efficiency, unsurpassed, in my judgment, in ancient or modern times. We have not been able to rival it, nor has there been any near approximation to it in the other rebel armies."

The cavalry force was small, but energetic and enterprising to a degree as yet by no means equalled by our own. The artillery was neither as good, nor as well equipped or served, as ours, but was commanded with intelligence, and able to give a good account of itself.

V.

DIFFICULTY OF AN ATTACK.

A N attack of Lee's position in front, even had Burn side's experience not demonstrated its folly, seemed to promise great loss of life without corresponding success.

To turn his right flank required the moving of pontoon trains and artillery over the worst of roads for at least twenty miles, through a country cut up by a multitude of streams running across the route to be taken, and emptying into either the Potomac or Rappahannock ; all requiring more or less bridging.

Lee's spy system was excellent. It has been claimed in Southern reports, that his staff had deciphered our signal code by watching a station at Stafford. And Butterfield admits this in one of his despatches of May 3. He would speedily ascertain any such movement, and could create formidable intrenchments on one side the river, as fast as we could build or repair roads on which to move down, upon the other. Moreover, there was a thousand feet of stream to bridge at the first available place below Skenker's Neck.

There remained nothing to do but to turn Lee's left

flank; and this could only be accomplished by stratagem, for Lee had strengthened every part of the river by which Hooker could attempt a passage.

But this problem was, despite its difficulties, still possible of solution; and Hooker set himself to work to elucidate it.

So soon as he had matured his plan, which he elaborated with the greatest care, but kept perfectly secret from every one until the movements themselves developed it, although making use of the knowledge and skill of all his generals both before and during its initiation, he speedily prepared for its vigorous execution. In May, the term of service of some twenty-two thousand nine-months and two-years men would expire. These men he must seek to utilize in the campaign.

The first intimation of a forward movement received by the army at large, apart from the Cavalry Corps, had been a circular of April 13, notifying commanding officers to have their troops supplied with eight days' rations, and a hundred and fifty rounds of ammunition, sixty to be carried by the soldiers, and the balance on the pack-mules.

After the battle of Fredericksburg, the army had returned to substantially the same positions and quarters occupied before; and here the men had housed themselves for the winter. The Mud March had broken up these cantonments; but after a few days' absence the several regiments returned to their old camps, and the same huts had generally been re-occupied by the same men. But when Fighting Joe Hooker's orders to march were issued, no one dreamed of any thing but victory; and the Army of the Potomac burned its ships. Nothing was left standing but the mud walls from which the shelter-tent roofs had been stripped, and an occasional chimney. Many of the men (though contrary to orders) set fire to what was left, and the *animus non revertendi* was as universal as the full confidence that now there lay before the Army of the Potomac a certain road, whatever might bar the path, to the long-wished-for goal of Richmond.

VI.

THE PROPOSED CAVALRY RAID.

HOOKER proposed to open his flank attack by cutting Lee's communications. Accordingly, on April 12, Gen. Stoneman, commanding the Cavalry Corps, received orders to march at seven A.M. next day, with his whole force except one brigade. He was to ascend the Rappahannock, keeping well out of view, and masking his movement with numerous small detachments, — alleging a chase of Jones's guerillas in the Shenandoah valley, as his objective. The river was to be crossed west of the Orange and Alexandria Railroad. At Culpeper he was to destroy or disperse Fitz Lee's brigade of some two thousand cavalry, and at Gordonsville the infantry provost-guard; thence to push down the Virginia Central to the Fredericksburg and Richmond Railroad, destroying every thing along the road. As the enemy would probably retreat by the latter route, he was to select strong points on the roads parallel to it, intrench, and hold his ground as obstinately as possible. If Lee retreated towards Gordonsville, he was to harass him day and night. The Confederates had but five thousand sabres to oppose him. " Let your watchword be, Fight! and let all your orders be, Fight, *Fight*, FIGHT!" exclaimed enthusi-astic Joe Hooker in this order. The primary object was to keep the Confederates from retreating to Richmond; and Stoneman was to rely on Hooker's being up with him in six days, or before his supplies were exhausted. If pos-sible, he was to detach at the most available points parties to destroy every thing in the direction of Charlottesville, and of the Pamunkey.

The Cavalry Corps, except Pleasonton's brigade, which accompanied Hooker's headquarters during this move-ment, left on the 13th. On the 15th Stoneman threw a division across the river at Rappahannock station, where the Orange and Alexandria Railroad crosses the river. But a sudden rise in consequence of heavy rains obliged this division to return by swimming the horses. Gen. Lee says, referring to this check, that "their efforts to establish themselves on the south side of the river were successfully resisted by Stuart." But the rise in the river was the actual cause. There was no crossing of swords.

At the time the cavalry marched, an infantry brigade and a battery were sent to Kelley's Ford, and a regiment to United-States Ford, to hold these crossings against scouting parties, or any counter-demonstration on the part of the enemy.

The river did not fall so that Stoneman could pass at that point until the 27th, when it was too late to accom-plish valuable results under the orders of the 12th; for the whole army was now on the march. Between the 15th and 27th the cavalry, under instructions from Hooker, re-mained in camp along the Orange and Alexandria Railroad.

It has, however, never been satisfactorily explained why it might not have crossed higher up, and have utilized these precious two weeks. It could not have been of less use than it was, and might possibly have been able to call Stuart's entire force away from Lee's army. Nor was it impossible, in part at least, to do the work cut out for it. Even to threaten Lee's communications would have seriously affected the singleness of purpose he displayed in this campaign.

But the operations of Stoneman, as they had no effect whatever upon the manœuvres of either Lee or Hooker, may be treated of separately, as a matter almost apart from the one under consideration.

And thus, in the failure of the cavalry raid, miscarried the first effort of this ill-fated campaign.

It is not often that the danger of detaching the entire cavalry force of an army, for service at a distance from its infantry corps, is illustrated in so marked a manner as it was on this occasion. Hooker left himself but a small brigade, of four regiments and a horse-battery, to do the scouting for an army of over one hundred thousand men. Had he retained a sufficient force to march with the main body, there would no doubt have been at least a brigade of it, instead of a few scouts, sent out to near Old Wilderness Tavern and along the Orange plank road to the junction of the Brock road. Jackson's movements would then have been fully known.

The bulk of the cavalry of an army should be with the infantry corps when in the presence of the enemy. For cavalry are the antennæ of an army.

VII.

THE FEINT BY THE LEFT WING.

GEN. HOOKER'S plan embraced, besides a cavalry raid to sever the enemy's communications, a demonstration in force on the left to draw the enemy's attention, and the throwing of the main body of his forces across the river on the right.

As early as April 21, Doubleday of the First Corps had been sent down the river to Port Conway with some thirty-five hundred men, to light camp-fires, and make demonstrations with pontoons, after doing which he returned to camp. On the 23d Col. Morrow, with the Twenty-fourth Michigan, went down, and crossed the river to Port Royal in boats.

These demonstrations had been intended to co-operate with Stoneman's raid, which at these dates should have been well on Lee's rear, and to unsettle Lee's firm footing preparatory to the heavy blows Hooker was preparing to deliver; but, as Stoneman was delayed, these movements failed of much of their intended effect. Nevertheless, Jackson's corps was drawn down to the vicinity, and remained there some days.

On Monday, April 27, Hooker issues his orders to

the First, Third, and Sixth Corps, to place themselves in position, ready to cross; the First at Pollock's Mills Creek, and the Sixth at Franklin's Crossing, by 3.30 A.M., on Wednesday; and the Third at a place enabling it to cross in support of either of the others at 4.30 A.M. The troops to remain concealed until the movement begins. Artillery to be posted by Gen. Hunt, Chief of Artillery of the army, to protect the crossing. Gen. Benham to have two bridges laid by 3.30 A.M. at each crossing. Troops, as needed, to be detailed to aid his engineer brigade.

Gen. Sedgwick to command the three corps, and make a demonstration in full force on Wednesday morning to secure the telegraph road. Should any considerable force be detached to meet the movement of the right wing, Sedgwick is to carry the works at all hazards. Should the enemy retreat towards Richmond, he is to pursue on the Bowling-Green road, fighting wherever he reaches them, while Hooker will pursue on parallel roads more to the west.

This order was punctually obeyed. Gen. Hunt placed forty-two guns at Franklin's, forty at Pollock's Mill, and sixteen at Traveller's Rest, a mile below, a number more being held in reserve. Those in position were so disposed as to "enfilade the rifle-pits, crush the fire of the enemy's works on the hill, cover the throwing of the bridges, and protect the crossing of the troops." (*Hunt.*)

These three corps camped that night without fires, and the pontoons were carried to the river by hand to insure secrecy.

At daybreak, Wednesday, Russell's brigade crossed in

boats at Franklin's with little opposition. The bridges were then constructed; and Brooks's division passed over with a battery, and established itself strongly on the south side.

At the lower crossing, Reynolds's attempts to throw the bridges early in the morning were defeated by sharp-shooters and a supporting regiment. But about half-past eight, the fog, which had been quite dense, lifted; and under fire of the artillery the Confederates were driven away, and the crossing made by Wadsworth.

During Wednesday and Thursday the entire command was held in readiness to force a passage at any time, the bridge-heads being held by Brooks and Wadsworth respectively.

VIII.

THE REAL MOVE BY THE RIGHT WING.

HOOKER was a master of logistics. The forethought and excellent judgment displayed in all orders under which these preliminary moves of the army-corps were made, as well as the high condition to which he had brought the army, cannot elicit higher praise than to state the fact, that, with the exception of the Cavalry Corps, all orders issued were carried out *au pied de la lettre*, and that each body of troops was on hand at the hour and place prescribed. This eulogy must, however, be confined to orders given prior to the time when the fighting began.

On April 26 the commanding officers of the Eleventh and Twelfth Corps were directed to march Monday morning, the 27th, towards Kelley's Ford, on the Rappahannock, — some fifteen miles above its junction with the Rapidan, — Howard leading.

As much secrecy as possible was enjoined, and the men were not to be allowed to go down to the river. Eight days' rations to be carried in the haversacks. Each corps to take a battery and two ambulances to a division, the pack-train for small ammunition, and a few wagons for forage only. The rest of the trains to be parked in the

32

vicinity of Banks's Ford out of sight. A sufficient detail, to be made from the troops whose term was about to expire, to be left behind to guard camp, and do provost duty.

Meade was ordered to march the Fifth Corps in connection with the Eleventh and Twelfth, and equipped in similar manner.

The three corps to be in camp at Kelley's Ford, in positions indicated, by four P.M. on Tuesday.

The first day's march was to the vicinity of Hartwood Church. Next day, at four A.M., the head of the column was in motion; and at four P.M. the three corps were in camp at Kelley's Ford.

At six P.M. the pontoon-bridge was begun, under charge of Capt. Comstock of the engineers, by a detail mostly from the Eleventh Corps. Some four hundred men of Buschbeck's brigade crossed in boats, and attacked the enemy's pickets, which retired after firing a single shot. About ten P.M. the bridge was finished, and the troops crossed; the Eleventh Corps during the night, and the Twelfth Corps next morning. The Seventeenth Pennsylvania Cavalry Regiment was sent out as flankers to prevent the Confederate scouting-parties from annoying the column. In this they failed of entire success; as the rear of the Eleventh Corps was, during the day, shelled by a Confederate battery belonging to Stuart's horse artillery, and the Twelfth Corps had some slight skirmishing in its front with cavalry detachments from the same command.

As soon as Hooker had seen to the execution of his first

orders, he transferred his headquarters to Morrisville, five miles north of Kelley's Ford, and superintended the execution of the crossing and advance. Urging Meade to equal celerity and secrecy in uncovering United-States Ford, he instructed Slocum, should Meade's crossing at Ely's be resisted, to push a column on the south side of the Rapidan to open the latter ford.

At Germania Ford, on the Rapidan, previously seized by an advance party of three or four smart marching regiments, a small body of one hundred and twenty-five Confederate infantry, guarding the supplies for the rebuilding of the bridge, then in progress, was captured.

The cavalry and artillery crossed at once by the ford, as well as a portion of the infantry, the latter wading almost to the armpits. But the construction of the bridge was soon temporarily completed by Gens. Geary and Kane; and the rest of the troops and the pack-mules passed safely, by the light of huge bonfires lighted on the banks. The men were in the highest possible spirits, and testified to their enjoyment of the march by the utmost hilarity.

At daylight the Twelfth Corps led the column, Geary in advance. Near the Wilderness, the head of column was attacked from the south by some cavalry and a couple of guns. Stuart had come up from Raccoon Ford the day previous. But a slight demonstration cleared the road; and Stuart retired, sending part of his force to Fredericksburg, and accompanying the rest to Spotsylvania Court House.

About two P.M., Thursday, these two corps, under command of Slocum, reached Chancellorsville, and found a portion of the Fifth Corps already in position there. The Twelfth Corps was deployed south of the plank road, with left at the Chancellor House, and the right near Wilderness Church, which line the Eleventh Corps prolonged to the vicinity of Hunting Creek.

The Fifth Corps had marched to Kelley's Ford, and crossed in rear of the Twelfth Corps. From here, Sykes's and Griffin's divisions marched towards Ely's Ford, preceded by Col. Devin's Sixth New York Cavalry, which surprised the pickets at that place. The troops crossed by wading. Humphreys remained behind to cover the passage of the trains, and after followed the column.

On crossing the Rapidan, Sykes was pushed towards United-States Ford, to dislodge the Confederate force there, by thus taking in reverse their position, while Griffin marched to Chancellorsville. The whole corps soon after united at the latter place, and was located with its right joining Slocum, and the left extending towards the river, facing Mine Run.

A skirmish of no particular moment had occurred between Griffin and Anderson, as the former reached Chancellorsville. Anderson had been retiring before the Federal advance, on the plank road towards Fredericksburg. His rear guard made a short stand at the cross-roads, but withdrew after a few rounds; and Anderson took up a position near Mine Road, where numerous ravines, perpendicular to the river, afforded excellent successive lines of defence.

On reaching Chancellorsville, Slocum took command of the three corps there assembled. He was ordered to ascertain, by a cavalry party, whether the enemy were detaching any considerable force from Fredericksburg to meet his column. If not, an advance at all hazards was to be made, and a position on the plank road which would uncover Banks's Ford to be secured. If the enemy were in strong force, Slocum was to select a position, and compel his attack. Not a moment was to be lost until the troops were concentrated at Chancellorsville. "From that moment all will be ours," said Hooker.

The inconsistency of these orders can be explained only by marked ignorance of the country. To secure a position which would uncover Banks's Ford was certainly a great desideratum; but the possession of Chancellorsville was far from accomplishing this end, as we shall see.

So admirably planned and executed were all orders up to this time, that on Thursday, by two P.M., three corps of nearly forty thousand men were concentrated on Lee's flank, while the latter was still unaware of the presence of any considerable Federal force in this vicinity.

On Monday Couch had been ordered to march two divisions of his (Second) corps to Banks' Ford, but to keep back from the river, and to show no more than the usual pickets. One brigade and a battery to be sent to United-States Ford, there to relieve an equal detail of the Eleventh Corps, which would rejoin its command. All their artillery to move with these two divisions, and to be ready to cover a forced crossing. The division whose camps at Falmouth were most easily seen by the enemy from across the river (it happened to be Gibbon's) to be left in camp to do picket and provost duty. The Third

Corps would be available in case the enemy himself attempted a crossing. Gibbon to be ready to join the command at any time.

On Thursday, as soon as Anderson withdrew Mahone's and Posey's brigades from United-States Ford, which he did when Meade's crossing at Ely's had flanked that position, Couch, whose bridge was all ready to throw, was ordered to cross, and march in support towards the heaviest firing. This he did, with French and Hancock, and reached Chancellorsville the same evening.

Swinton, rather grandiloquently, says, " To have marched a column of fifty thousand men, laden with sixty pounds of baggage and encumbered with artillery and trains, thirty-seven miles in two days; to have bridged and crossed two streams, guarded by a vigilant enemy, with the loss of half a dozen men, one wagon, and two mules, — is an achievement which has few parallels, and which well deserves to rank with Prince Eugene's famous passage of the Adige."

However exaggerated this praise may be, Hooker nevertheless deserves high encomiums on his management of the campaign so far. Leaving Stoneman's delay out of the question, nothing had gone wrong or been mismanaged up to the present moment. But soon Hooker makes his first mistake.

At 12.30 P.M. on Thursday, the Third Corps, which lay near Franklin's Crossing, on the north side of the river, received orders to proceed by the shortest route, and concealed from the enemy, to United-States Ford, to be across the river by seven A.M., Friday; in pursuance of which order, Sickles immediately started, in three columns, following the ravines to Hamet's, at the intersection of the Warrenton pike and United-States Ford road. Here he bivouacked for the night. At five A.M. Friday he marched to the ford, and passed it with the head of his column at seven A.M., Birney leading, Whipple and Berry in the rear. Leaving Mott's brigade and a battery to protect the trains at the ford, he then pushed on, and reported at Chancellorsville at nine A.M. Under Hooker's orders he massed his corps near the junction of the roads to Ely's and United-States Fords, in the open near Bullock's, sending a brigade and a battery to Dowdall's Tavern.

Hooker, meanwhile, had arrived at Chancellorsville, and taken command. He at once issued this characteristic order : —

HEADQUARTERS ARMY OF THE POTOMAC,
CAMP NEAR FALMOUTH, VA., April 30, 1863.
GENERAL ORDERS, NO. 47.

It is with heartfelt satisfaction that the commanding general announces to the army that the operations of the last three days have determined that our enemy must ingloriously fly, or come out from behind his defences, and give us battle on our own ground, where certain destruction awaits him.

The operations of the Fifth, Eleventh, and Twelfth Corps have been a succession of splendid achievements.

By command of Major-Gen. Hooker.

S. WILLIAMS,
Assistant Adjutant-General.

Pleasonton, during Thursday, pushed out towards Fredericksburg and Spotsylvania Court House to observe the enemy.

Fitz Hugh Lee had bivouacked this evening at Todd's Tavern. Stuart, with his staff, had started towards Fredericksburg to report the condition of affairs to Gen. Lee. It was a bright moonlight night. A mile or two on the road he ran against a party of Federal horsemen, the advance of the Sixth New York Cavalry, under Lieut.-Col. McVicar. Sending back for the Fifth Virginia Cavalry, Lee attacked the Federal troopers, leading in person at the head of his staff; but, being repulsed, he sent for the entire brigade to come up, with which he drove back McVicar's detachment.

The combat lasted some time, and was interesting as being a night affair, in which the naked weapon was freely used. Its result was to prevent Pleasonton from reaching Spotsylvania Court House, where he might have destroyed a considerable amount of stores.

The position on Thursday evening was then substantially this. At Hamilton's Crossing there was no change. Each party was keenly scanning the movements of the other, seeking to divine his purpose. Sedgwick and Reynolds were thus holding the bulk of Lee's army at and near Fredericksburg. Hooker, with four corps, and Sickles close by, lay at Chancellorsville, with only Anderson's small force in his front, and with his best chances hourly slipping away. For Lee, by this time aware of the real situation, hesitated not a moment in the measures to be taken to meet the attack of his powerful enemy.

IX.

LEE'S INFORMATION AND MOVEMENTS.

L ET us now turn to Lee, and see what he has been doing while Hooker thus discovered check.

Pollard says: "Lee calmly watched this" (Sedgwick's) "movement, as well as the one higher up the river under Hooker, until he had penetrated the enemy's design, and seen the necessity of making a rapid division of his own forces, to confront him on two different fields, and risking the result of fighting him in detail."

Lossing states Lee's object as twofold: to retain Banks's Ford, so as to divide Hooker's army, and to keep his right wing in the Wilderness.

Let us listen to Lee himself. In his report he says he was convinced on Thursday, as Sedgwick continued inactive, that the main attack would be made on his flank and rear. "The strength of the force which had crossed, and its apparent indisposition to attack, indicated that the principal effort of the enemy would be made in some other quarter."

He states that on April 14 he was informed that Federal cavalry was concentrating on the upper Rappahannock. On the 21st, that small bodies of infantry had appeared at Kelley's Ford. These movements, and the demonstrations at Port Royal, "were evidently intended to conceal the designs of the enemy," who was about to resume active operations.

The Federal pontoon bridges and troops below Fredericksburg " were effectually protected from our artillery by the depth of the river's bed and the narrowness of the stream, while the batteries on the other side completely commanded the wide plain between our lines and the river."

" As at the first battle of Fredericksburg, it was thought best to select positions with a view to resist the advance of the enemy, rather than incur the heavy loss that would attend any attempt to prevent his crossing."

At the time of Hooker's flank movement, there were between the Rappahannock and Rapidan no troops excepting some twenty-seven hundred cavalry under Stuart, forming Lee's extreme left. But Stuart made up for his small numbers by his promptness in conveying to his chief information of every movement and of the size of every column during Hooker's passage of the rivers. And the capture of a few prisoners from each of the Fifth, Eleventh, and Twelfth Corps enabled him and his superior to gauge the dimensions of the approaching army with fair accuracy.

But until Thursday night the plan of Hooker's attack was not sufficiently developed to warrant decisive action on the part of Lee.

Of the bulk of the Confederate forces, Early's division was ahead at Hamilton's Crossing, intrenched in an almost impregnable position.   On Wednesday, April 29, the rest of Jackson's corps was moved up from below, where Doubleday's and Morrow's demonstrations had until now kept it.

A. P. Hill's and Trimble's divisions were in the second and third lines on this wing; while Anderson and McLaws, the only troops of Longstreet's corps left with the Army of Northern Virginia, held the intrenchments along the river above Fredericksburg.   Barksdale was in the town. Pendleton with the reserve artillery was at Massaponax.

When, from Sedgwick's inactivity and the information received from Stuart, Lee, on Wednesday afternoon, had been led to suspect that the main attack might be from the columns crossing above, he had immediately ordered Anderson to occupy Chancellorsville with Wright's brigade, and with Mahone and Posey from United-States Ford, so soon as that position was compromised, leaving a few companies there to dispute its possession as long as possible.

We have seen how Anderson engaged Meade near Chancellorsville as the latter advanced, and then retired to a position near Mine-Run road.   Here was the crest of a hill running substantially north and south.   Gen. Lee had already selected this line; and Col. Smith, his chief engineer, had drawn up a plan of intrenchments.   Anderson detailed men, who, during the night, threw up some strong field-works.

Late Thursday night Lee appears first fully to have matured his plan for parrying Hooker's thrust.

Barksdale's brigade was left at Fredericksburg, where

during the winter it had been doing picket-duty, to form the left of the line remaining to oppose Sedgwick. Part of Pendleton's reserve artillery was near by; while Early, commanding this entire body, held Hamilton's Crossing. He had a force of eighty-five hundred muskets, and thirty pieces of artillery.

The rest of his army Lee at once took well in hand, and moved out to meet the Army of the Potomac. McLaws was hurried forward to sustain the line taken up by Anderson. He arrived on the ground by daylight of Friday, and went into position in rifle-pits on the right about Smith's Hill.

Jackson, equally alert, but having a longer distance to march from the extreme right along the military road, arrived about eight A.M., took command, and, as was his wont, ordered an immediate advance, throwing Owens's regiment of cavalry forward to reconnoitre.

Posey and Wright followed Owens on the plank road, with Alexander's battalion of artillery. Mahone, and Jordan's battery detached from Alexander, marched abreast of his right, on the pike.

McLaws followed Mahone, and Wilcox and Perry were called from Banks's Ford to sustain this column, which McLaws directed; while Jackson, following on the plank road, watched the operations of the left.

X.

HOOKER'S ADVANCE FRIDAY.

SO far the headquarters of the Army of the Potomac had been at Falmouth, where still remained Gen. Butterfield, Hooker's chief of staff. The last order from this point had been on Thursday to Gen. Sedgwick, who was therein notified that headquarters would be that night at Chancellorsville; that an advance would be made Friday morning along the plank road (meaning probably the pike) towards Fredericksburg, to uncover Banks's Ford, thus making a shorter communication through Butterfield, who would still remain at Falmouth. This order substantially recapitulates former instructions, and is full of the flash and *vim* of an active mind, till then intent on its work and abreast of the situation. It urges on Sedgwick co-operation with the right wing, and the most vigorous pushing of the enemy. It impresses on him that both wings will be within easy communication, and ready to spring to one another's assistance.

Slower than his adversary, and failing to follow up with vigor his advantage already gained, Hooker assumes command in person, and reconnoitres the ground between himself and Fredericksburg. He then orders Meade, with

44

Griffin, followed by Humphreys, and with three batteries, to march along the river road to some commanding point between Mott and Colin Runs; his advance to be masked by throwing out small parties, and his command to be in position by two P.M.; while Sykes's division, supported by Hancock's division of the Second Corps, march out the turnpike to a corresponding distance, each force then deploying towards the other, and engaging the enemy supposed to be in that vicinity.

A third column, consisting of the Twelfth Corps, he orders to march by the plank road, and to be massed near Tabernacle Church, masked in like manner; to be in position by midday, so that the Eleventh Corps can move up to take position a mile in its rear as reserve, by two P.M.

French's division of the Second Corps, and one battery, are ordered to Todd's Tavern, from which detachments are to be thrown out on the various roads.

The unemployed troops are massed at Chancellorsville, out of the roads. Pleasonton holds his cavalry brigade there in readiness to move. Hooker announces his headquarters at Tabernacle Church as soon as the movement opens.

Immediately after (11.30 A.M., Friday,) Sedgwick is directed to threaten an attack at one P.M., in the direction of Hamilton's Crossing, to ascertain whether the enemy is hugging his defences in full force. A corps is to be used with proper supports, but nothing more than a demonstration to be made. If certain that the enemy is there in force, Sedgwick is to make no attack.

Sedgwick did not receive this order until about five

P.M., but nevertheless made a display in force of Reynolds's corps, with Newton and Brooks in support. But a countermand was soon received, and the troops withdrawn.

As Hooker supposed his enemy to be in line somewhere midway between Chancellorsville and Fredericksburg, the purpose of these orders to Sedgwick is not plain. Meade, Sykes, and Slocum were ordered to attack the enemy when met. Sedgwick could aid such an attack by pushing the force in his front at Hamilton's. But a mere demonstration to find out whether the heights were strongly held could have no effect upon the real advance, nor procure Hooker any timely information.

The movement of the three columns out of the Wilderness begins at eleven A.M. It is in accordance with the declared plans of Hooker, and with sound policy. For Chancellorsville is of all places the worst in which to deliver or accept a general engagement, and every mile's advance towards Fredericksburg brings the army into more open ground.

Meade, with Griffin and Humphreys, advances on the river road to within a short distance of Banks's Ford, near Decker's farm. He can easily seize the ford, the possession of which lessens the distance between the wings by six miles. It is the objective Hooker has had in view ever since the movement began. He is preparing to deploy towards Sykes.

Sykes, — to quote Warren, — " on gaining the ridge about a mile and a quarter from Chancellorsville, found the enemy advancing, and driving back our cavalry. This small force resisted handsomely, riding up and firing almost in the faces of the Eleventh Virginia Infantry, which formed the enemy's advance. Gen. Sykes moved forward in double-quick time, attacked the enemy vigorously, and drove him back with loss, till he had gained the position assigned him."

This is a crest in front of the heavy forest, and in range of Anderson's rifle-pits. The Federal skirmishers are the Seventeenth United-States Infantry, supported by Burbank's brigade.

McLaws is in his front, and deploys across the pike, Semmes on the left of the road, Mahone, Perry, and Wofford on the right. Jordan's battery is posted on the Mine road.

Sykes brings up Weed's battery, and opens on Semmes, and drives in his skirmishers, but can make no serious impression on his line. McLaws sends word to Jackson that Sykes is attacking in force, and that the country is favorable for a flank attack.

Jackson orders Kershaw through the woods to join Semmes's left, and sends Wilcox up the Mine road to extend the Confederate right, and head off a Federal advance from this direction.

Sykes thus finds himself overlapped on both flanks. He throws Ayres's regular brigade out on his left, and the One Hundred and Forty-sixth New York on his right. His position is difficult, but he determines to hold it as long as possible.

It is noon. No sounds are heard from the parallel columns. Sykes has to make his line very thin, but holds his ground. If supported, he can maintain himself.

But at this juncture he receives orders to fall back on Chancellorsville, and slowly retires to McGee's; later to his old position, Hancock taking his place in the front line; and he next morning at daylight is also withdrawn, and takes up the line he retains until Sunday morning.

Slocum, in like manner on the plank road, meets Posey and Wright, and a small affair occurs. But Wright is sent along the unfinished railroad, and outflanks him. He is also at this moment ordered to retire.

Meade has had similar orders, and has likewise withdrawn; and Wilcox is sent to Banks's Ford to hold it.

Wright continues his movement along the railroad, as far as Welford's or Catherine's Furnace, when, finding himself beyond communication with his superior, he, in connection with Stuart, who has been holding this point, determines to feel the Union line. Two regiments and a battery are thrown in along the road to Dowdall's Tavern, preceded by skirmishers. Our pickets fall back, and through the dense wood the Confederates reach our line. But they are warmly received, and retire. This is six P.M. Wright now joins his division.

Lee has arrived, and assumes command.

Jackson's divisions, thus following up our retiring columns, by nightfall occupy a line from Mine road to Welford's Furnace. A regiment of cavalry is on the Mine road, and another on the river road as outposts. Stuart remains at the Furnace. McLaws occupies the crest east of Big-Meadow Swamp, and Anderson prolongs his lines westwardly.

Let us now examine into these operations of Friday.

This movement towards Fredericksburg was not a sudden idea of Hooker's, but the result of a carefully studied plan. In his order of April 3, to Sedgwick, he says that he proposes to assume the initiative, advance along the plank road, and uncover Banks's Ford, and at once throw bridges across. Gen. Butterfield, in a communication to Sedgwick of April 30, says, " He (Hooker) expected when he left here, if he met with no serious opposition, to be on the heights west of Fredericksburg to-morrow noon or shortly after, and, if opposed strongly, to-morrow night." In his testimony before the Committee on the Conduct of the War, Hooker says, " The problem was, to throw a sufficient force of infantry across at Kelley's Ford, descend the Rappahannock, and knock away the enemy's forces, holding the United-States and Banks's Ford, by attacking them in the rear, and as soon as these fords were opened, to re-enforce the marching column sufficiently for them to continue the march upon the flank of the rebel army until his whole force was routed, and, if successful, his retreat intercepted. Simultaneous with this movement on the right, the left was to cross the Rappahannock below Fredericksburg, and threaten the enemy in that quarter, including his depot of supplies, to prevent his detaching an overwhelming force to his left."

Hooker, moreover, not only told Hunt that he expected to fight near Banks's Ford, but instructed him to get all his artillery to that point from below, where it had been massed to cover Sedgwick's crossing.

There was every reason why the army should be got out of the Wilderness, in the midst of which lies Chancellors-

ville.   This is, of all places in that section, the least fit for
an engagement in which the general commanding expects
to secure the best tactical results.   But out towards Fredericksburg the ground opens, showing a large number of
clearings, woods of less density, and a field suited to the
operations of all arms.

Every thing should have been done to get the two
wings within easier communication; and more than all,
having once surprised the enemy, and advanced against
him, a retreat should have been made from imperative
reasons alone.

Hooker explains this falling back in after-days, before
the Committee on the Conduct of the War, thus: "They"
— the forces on the turnpike and plank road — "had proceeded but a short distance when the head of the column
emerged from the heavy forest, and discovered the enemy
to be advancing in line of battle.   Nearly all the Twelfth
Corps had emerged from the forest at that moment" (this
is a very imperfect statement of the facts); "but, as the
passage-way through the forest was narrow, I was satisfied
that I could not throw troops through it fast enough to
resist the advance of Gen. Lee, and was apprehensive of
being whipped in detail."   And in another place, "When
I marched out on the morning of the 1st of May I could
get but few troops into position: the column had to march
through narrow roads, and could not be thrown forward
fast enough to prevent their being overwhelmed by the
enemy in his advance.   On assuming my position, Lee
advanced on me in that manner, and was soon repulsed,
the column thrown back in confusion into the open

ground. It could not live there. The roads through the
forest were not unlike bridges to pass. A mile or more
in advance of the position I had would have placed me
beyond the forest, where, with my superior forces, the
enemy would in all probability have been beaten."

This was not a valid conclusion from the actual facts.
Listen to his subordinates' statements.

Gen. Humphreys testifies before the Committee on the
Conduct of the War, with reference to this falling-back:
" It was totally unexpected to me : I thought it was part
of the plan to attack him as quickly as possible. We had
surprised them, and were strong enough to attack them."
" After Friday I was apprehensive we should not have the
success we had expected." " I think it was a mistake to
fight a defensive battle after surprising the enemy." "I
think we should have attacked the enemy immediately."
" I must give my opinion, since you ask me ; for I have an
opinion, as a military man, from the general facts I know,
and that I suppose I am obliged to express. My opinion
is, that we should not have been withdrawn, called back,
on Friday afternoon. We had advanced along the road
to Fredericksburg to attack the enemy : the troops were
in fine spirits, and we wanted to fight a battle. I think
we ought to have fought the enemy there. They came
out, and attacked one division of the corps I belonged to,
just at the time we returned to Chancellorsville. What
caused Gen. Hooker to return after advancing some miles
on this general position, which was about perpendicular to
the plank road leading to Fredericksburg, I am not able
to say, because, being only a division commander, the

facts were not stated to me. But I have heard it said that he received some erroneous information about the enemy's advancing on his flank from the direction of Orange Court House. It was my opinion, we should have attacked the enemy, instead of withdrawing, and awaiting an attack from the enemy."

He also testifies, that, after the troops were ordered back to Chancellorsville, they were for many hours massed there in considerable confusion, until, after a deal of counter-marching, they were got into place.

Pleasonton states that the retreat from open ground "produced among the soldiers a feeling of uncertainty."

Hancock testified before the Committee on the Conduct of the War: "I consider the mistake in the matter was in even stopping at Chancellorsville. . . . I believe, if all . . . had pushed right down to Banks's Ford, the whole movement would have been a perfect success. But I have no doubt that we ought to have held our advance positions, and still kept pushing on, and attempt to make a junction with Gen. Sedgwick."

Gen. Warren, whose whole testimony and report are the clearest and most useful of all the evidence obtainable from any single source, on this campaign, suggested to Couch, who was supporting Sykes on Friday, when the latter was attacked by Jackson, to delay carrying out Hooker's orders to retire, while he (Warren) galloped back to headquarters to explain the importance of holding the position, which was formidable and had great tactical advantages. Hooker yielded; but, before Warren could get back to the front, the previous orders had been obeyed, and the position lost. He says: "I never should have stopped at Chancellorsville. I should have advanced and fought the enemy, instead of waiting for him to attack me. The character of the country was the great reason for advancing."

And it is thought that every one engaged in this campaign with the Army of the Potomac will remember the feeling of confusion and uncertainty engendered by the withdrawal from Jackson's front on this unlucky day.

A council of general officers was held at Chancellorsville on Friday evening, in which many were still strongly in favor of making the advance again. Warren says: "I was in favor of advancing, and urged it with more zeal than convincing argument." But Hooker held to his own opinion. He could not appreciate the weakness of assuming the defensive in the midst of the *élan* of a successful advance.

It is not difficult to state what Hooker should have done. He had a definite plan, which was to uncover and use Banks's Ford. He should have gone on in the execution of this plan until arrested by superior force, or until something occurred to show that his plan was inexpedient. To retire from an enemy whom you have gone out to attack, and whom you have already placed at a disadvantage, before striking a blow, is weak generalship indeed.

Hooker had arrived at Chancellorsville at noon Thursday. Lee was still in Fredericksburg. The troops were able to march many miles farther without undue taxing. They should have been pushed out that afternoon to the open ground and to Banks's Ford. To fail in this, was the first great error of the campaign. There had not been a moment's delay allowed from the time the troops reached the river until they were massed at Chancellorsville, and the proposed movement nearly completed. One continued pressure, never let up, had constantly been exerted by the headquarters of the army. The troops had been kept in constant movement towards Banks's Ford. Hooker had all but reached his goal. Suddenly occurred a useless, unexplained pause of twenty-four hours. And it was during this unlucky gap of time that Lee occupied the ground which Hooker's cavalry could have seized, and which should have been held at all hazards.

Nor is this error excusable from ignorance of the *terrain.* For Hooker had shown his knowledge of the importance of celerity; and his own declared plan made Banks's Ford, still a half-dozen miles distant, his one objective. In his testimony before the Committee on the Conduct of the War, he thus refers to his plan: " As soon as Couch's divisions and Sykes's corps came up, I directed an advance for the purpose, in the first instance, of driving the enemy away from Banks's Ford, which was six miles down the river, in order that we might be in closer communication with the left wing of the army." And if the troops had needed repose, a few hours would have sufficed; and, the succeeding night being clear moonlight, a forward movement was then entirely feasible.

Dating from this delay of Thursday, every thing seemed to go wrong.

More curious still is Hooker's conduct on Friday, when

his three columns came into presence of the enemy. What every one would have expected of Fighting Joe was, that at this supreme moment his energy would have risen to its highest pitch. It was a slight task to hold the enemy for a few hours. Before ordering the columns back, Hooker should have gone in person to Sykes's front. Here he would have shortly ascertained that Jackson was moving around his right. What easier than to leave a strong enough force at the edge of the Wilderness, and to move by his left towards Banks's Ford, where he already had Meade's heavy column? This would have kept his line of communication with United-States Ford open, and, while uncovering Banks's Ford, would at the same time turn Jackson's right. It is not as if such a movement carried him away from his base, or uncovered his communications. It was the direct way to preserve both.

But at this point Hooker faltered. Fighting Joe had reached the culminating desire of his life. He had come face to face with his foe, and had a hundred and twenty thousand eager and well-disciplined men at his back. He had come to fight, and he — retreated without crossing swords.

XI.

THE POSITION AT CHANCELLORSVILLE.

THE position at Chancellorsville was good for neither attack nor defence. The ground was not open enough for artillery, except down the few roads, and across an occasional clearing. Cavalry was useless. Infantry could not advance steadily in line. The ground was such in Hooker's front, that Lee could manœuvre or mass his troops unseen by him. Our own troops were so located, that to re-enforce any portion of the line, which might be attacked, with sufficient speed, was impossible.

Anderson (as has been stated) had been ordered by Lee to hold Chancellorsville; but after examination of the ground, and consultation with Mahone and Posey, he concluded to transcend his instructions, and retired to the junction of Mine Road and the turnpike. He assumed that the superiority of this latter ground would excuse his failure to hold his position in the Wilderness.

Gen. Hancock says: "I consider that the position at Chancellorsville was not a good one. It was a flat country, and had no local military advantages."

And the testimony of all our general officers is strongly to the same effect.

The position to which Hooker retired was the same which the troops, wearied with their march of Thursday, had taken up without any expectation of fighting a battle there. Hooker had desired to contract his lines somewhat after Friday's check; but the feeling that farther retreat would still more dishearten the men, already wondering at this unexplained withdrawal, and the assurance of the generals on the right that they could hold it against any force the enemy could bring against their front, decided him in favor of leaving the line as it was, and of strengthening it by breastworks and abattis.

Having established his troops in position, Hooker further strengthened his right wing at Chancellorsville to the detriment of his left below Fredericksburg; and at 1.55 A.M., Saturday, ordered all the bridges at Franklin's Crossing, and below, to be taken up, and Reynolds's corps to march at once, with pack-train, to report at headquarters.

This corps reached him Saturday night, and was deployed upon the extreme right of the new position then being taken up by the army.

The line as now established lay as follows: —

Meade held the left, extending from a small bluff near Scott's Dam on the Rappahannock, and covering the roads on the river, along a crest between Mine and Mineral Spring Runs towards and within a short mile of Chancellorsville.

This crest was, however, commanded from several points on the east, and, according to the Confederate authorities, appeared to have been carelessly chosen. Meade's front, except at the extreme river-flank, was covered by impenetrable woods. The Mine road intersected his left flank, and the River road was parallel to and a mile in his front.

Couch joined Meade's right, and extended southerly to Chancellorsville, with Hancock thrown out on his front, and facing east, astride the River road, and up to and across the old turnpike; his line being formed south of this road and of the Chancellor clearing. The division of French, of Couch's corps, was held in reserve along the United-States Ford road.

From here to Dowdall's Tavern the line made a southerly sweep outwards, like a bent bow, of which the plank road was the string.

As far as Hazel Grove, at the centre of the bow, Slocum's Twelfth Corps held the line, Geary's division joining on to Couch, and Williams on the right. From Slocum's right to the extreme right of the army, the Eleventh Corps had at first been posted; but Hooker determined on Saturday morning that the line was too thin here, and thrust Birney's division of the Third Corps in between Slocum and Howard. The rest of the Third Corps was in reserve, massed in columns of battalions, in Bullock's clearing, north of the Chancellor house, with its batteries at the fork of the roads leading to the United-States and Ely's Fords.

Towards sunset of Friday, Birney had advanced a strong line of skirmishers, and seized a commanding position in his front. Birney's line then lay along the crest facing Scott's Run from Dowdall's to Slocum's right.

Pleasonton's cavalry brigade was massed at headquarters, ready for duty at any point.

Howard held the line, from Dowdall's Tavern (Melzi Chancellor's) to beyond Talley's farm on the old pike, with his right flank substantially in the air, and with two roads, the main thoroughfares from east to west, striking in on his right, parallel to his position.

As will be noticed from the map, the right, being along the pike, was slightly refused from the rest of the line, considering the latter as properly lying along the road to headquarters. From Dowdall's west, the rise along the pike was considerable, and at Talley's the crest was high. The whole corps lay on the watershed of the small tributaries of the Rappahannock and Mattapony Rivers.

As a position to resist a southerly attack, it was as good as the Wilderness afforded; although the extreme right rested on no obstacle which superiority in numbers could not overcome. And a heavy force, massed in the clearing at Dowdall's as a *point d'appui*, was indispensable to safety, inasmuch as the conformation of the ground afforded nothing for this flank to lean upon.

Having forfeited the moral superiority gained by his advance, having withdrawn to his intrenchments at Chancellorsville, and decided, after surprising his enemy, upon fighting a defensive battle, Hooker, early on Saturday morning, examined his lines, and made sundry changes in the forces under his command.

The position he occupied, according to Gen. Lee, was one of great natural strength, on ground covered with dense forest and tangled under-growth, behind breastworks of logs and an impenetrable abattis, and approached by few roads, all easily swept by artillery. And, while it is true that the position was difficult to carry by direct assault, full compensation existed in other tactical advantages to the army taking the offensive. It is not probable that Lee, in Hooker's place, would have selected such ground. " Once in the wood, it was difficult to tell any thing at one hundred yards. Troops could not march without inextricable confusion." Despite which fact, however, the density of these very woods was the main cause of Lee's success.

In this position, Hooker awaited the assault of his vigorous opponent. As in all defensive battles, he was at certain disadvantages, and peculiarly so in this case, owing to the *terrain* he had chosen, or been forced to choose by Friday's easily accepted check. There were no *debouches* for throwing forces upon Lee, should he wish to assume the offensive. There was no ground for manœuvring. The woods were like a heavy curtain in his front. His left wing was placed so as to be of absolutely no value. His right flank was in the air. One of the roads on which he must depend for retreat was readily assailable by the enemy. And he had in his rear a treacherous river, which after a few hours' rain might become impassable, with but a single road and ford secured to him with reasonable certainty.

And, prone as we had always been to act upon unwarrantable over-estimates of the strength of our adversaries, Hooker had not this reason to allege for having retired to await Lee's attack. For he had just received excellent information from Richmond, to the effect that Lee's rations amounted to fifty-nine thousand daily; and we have seen that he told Slocum, on Thursday, that his column of nearly forty thousand men was much stronger than any force Lee could detach against him. Hooker acknowledges as much in his testimony before the Committee on the Conduct of the War, when, in answer to the question, " What portion of the enemy lay between you and Gen. Sedgwick? " he replied : —

" Lee's army at Fredericksburg numbered sixty thousand, not including the artillery, cavalry, and the forces stationed up the river, occupying the posts at Culpeper and Gordonsville. I think my information on this point was reliable, as I had made use of unusual means to ascertain. The enemy left eight thousand men to occupy the lines about Fredericksburg; Jackson marched off to my right with twenty-five thousand; and Lee had the balance between me and Sedgwick."

It will be well to remember this acknowledgment, when we come to deal with Hooker's theories of the force in his own front on Sunday and Monday.

XII.

JACKSON'S MARCH, AND SICKLES'S ADVANCE.

LEE and Jackson spent Friday night under some pine-trees, on the plank road, at the point where the Confederate line crosses it. Lee saw that it was impossible for him to expect to carry the Federal lines by direct assault, and his report states that he ordered a cavalry reconnoissance towards our right flank to ascertain its position. There is, however, no mention of such a body having felt our lines on the right, in any of the Federal reports.

It is not improbable that Lee received information, crude but useful, about this portion of our army, from some women belonging to Dowdall's Tavern. When the Eleventh Corps occupied the place on Thursday, a watch was kept upon the family living there. But in the interval between the corps breaking camp to move out to Slocum's support on Friday morning, and its return to the old position, some of the women had disappeared. This fact was specially noted by Gen. Howard.

However the information was procured, the Federal right was doubtless ascertained to rest on high ground, where it was capable of making a stubborn resistance towards the south. But Lee well knew that its position was approached from the west by two broad roads, and reasoned justly that Hooker, in canvassing the events of Friday, would most probably look for an attack on his left or front.

Seated on a couple of cracker-boxes, the relics of an issue of Federal rations the day before, the two Confederate chieftains discussed the situation. Jackson, with characteristic restless energy, suggested a movement with his entire corps around Hooker's right flank, to seize United-States Ford, or fall unawares upon the Army of the Potomac. This hazardous suggestion, which Lee in his report does not mention as Jackson's, but which is universally ascribed to him by Confederate authorities, was one as much fraught with danger as it was spiced with dash, and decidedly bears the Jacksonian flavor. It gave "the great flanker" twenty-two thousand men (according to Col. A. S. Pendleton, his assistant adjutant-general, but twenty-six thousand by morning report) with which to make a march which must at best take all day, constantly exposing his own flank to the Federal assault. It separated for a still longer time the two wings of the Confederate army; leaving Lee with only Anderson's and McLaws's divisions, — some seventeen thousand men, — with which to resist the attack of thrice that number, which Hooker, should he divine this division of forces, could throw against him, the while he kept Jackson busy with the troops on his own right flank.

On the other hand, Hooker had shown clear intention of fighting a defensive battle; and perhaps Lee measured his man better than the Army of the Potomac had done. And he knew Jackson too. Should Hooker remain quiet during the day, either voluntarily or by Lee's engrossing his attention by constant activity in his front, the stratagem might succeed. And in case of failure, each wing had open ground and good roads for retreat, to form a junction towards Gordonsville.

Moreover, nothing better presented itself; and though, in the presence of a more active foe, Lee would never have hazarded so much, the very aggressiveness of the manœuvre, and the success of Jackson's former flank attacks, commended it to Lee, and he gave his lieutenant orders to proceed to its immediate execution.

For this division of his forces in the presence of an enemy of twice his strength, Lee is not entitled to commendation. It is justifiable only — if at all — by the danger of the situation, which required a desperate remedy, and peculiarly by the success which attended it. Had it resulted disastrously, as it ought to have done, it would have been a serious blow to Lee's military prestige. The "nothing venture, nothing have" principle applies to it better than any maxim of tactics.

Before daybreak Jackson sends two of his aides, in company with some local guides, to find a practicable road, by which he may, with the greatest speed and all possible secrecy, gain the position he aims at on Hooker's right and rear, and immediately sets his corps in motion, with Rodes, commanding D. H. Hill's division, in the advance, and A. P. Hill bringing up the rear.

Jackson's route lay through the woods, along the road

on which rested Lee's line. His corps, since Friday's manœuvres, was on the left; and, as he withdrew his troops at dawn, Lee deployed to the left to fill the gap, first placing Wright where Jackson had been on the west of the plank road, and later, when Wright was ordered to oppose Sickles at the Furnace, Mahone's brigade.

This wood-road led to Welford's or Catherine's Furnace, from which place a better one, called the Furnace road, zigzagged over to join the Brock (or Brook) road, the latter running northerly into Y-shaped branches, each of which intersected the pike a couple of miles apart.

Jackson was obliged to make some repairs to the road as he advanced, for the passage of his artillery and trains. In many places the bottom, none too reliable at any time, was so soft with the recent rains, that it had to be corduroyed to pull the guns through. But these men were used to marches of unequalled severity, and their love for their leader made no work too hard when " Old Jack " shared it with them. And although they had already been marching and fighting continuously for thirty hours, this circuit of well-nigh fifteen miles was cheerfully done, with an alacrity nothing but willing and courageous hearts, and a blind belief that they were outwitting their enemy, could impart.

His progress was masked by Stuart, who interposed his cavalry between Jackson and the Union lines, and constantly felt of our skirmishers and pickets as he slowly kept abreast with the marching column.

At the Furnace comes in another road, which, a short distance above, forks so as to lead to Dowdall's Tavern on the left, and to touch the Union lines by several other branches on the right. It was this road down which Wright and Stuart had advanced the evening before in their attack on our lines.

Here, in passing Lewis's Creek (Scott's Run) and some elevated ground near by, the column of Jackson had to file in full view of the Union troops, barely a mile and a half away. The movement was thus fully observed by us, hundreds of field-glasses pointing steadily at his columns.

It seems somewhat strange that Jackson should have made this march, intended to be quite disguised, across the Furnace-clearing. For there was another equally short route, making a bend southward through the woods, and, though possibly not so good as the one pursued, subsequently found available for the passage of Jackson's trains, when driven from the Furnace by Sickles. It is probably explained, however, by the fact that this route, selected during the night, was unfamiliar to Jackson, and that his aides and guides had not thought of the point where the troops were thus put *en évidence.* And Jackson may not have been with the head of the column.

So early as eight o'clock Birney of the Third Corps, whose division had been thrust in between Howard and Slocum, reported to Sickles that a movement in considerable force was being made in our front. Sickles conveyed the information to Hooker, who instructed him to investigate the matter in person. Sickles pushed out Clark's rifled battery, with a sufficient support, to shell the passing column. This, says Sickles, obliged it to abandon the road. It was observed that the column was a large one, and had a heavy train. Sickles considered it either a movement for attack on our right, or else one in retreat. If the former, he surmised at the time that he had arrested it; if the latter, that the column had taken a more available route.

It was while Rodes was filing past the Furnace that the first attack by Clark's battery was made; and Col. Best, with the Twenty-third Georgia Regiment, was sent out beyond the Furnace to hold the road. Best subsequently took position in and about the Furnace buildings, and placed some troops in the railroad cutting south.

Sickles, meanwhile, had again reported to Hooker, and been instructed to strengthen his reconnoissance. But it was noon before this order was given, and he was then advised to push out with great caution. He asked for the whole of Birney's division, and another one in support. With these he thought to get possession of the road on which the enemy was moving, and, if it was a retreat, cut him off; if a flank movement, thrust himself in between the two bodies of the enemy. Hooker accorded this request; and Birney was advanced a mile and a half through the woods, bridging two or three arms of Scott's Run, and some marshy ground, and making his way with great difficulty. Two regiments of Berdan's sharpshooters were thrown out in front, and the Twentieth Indiana Infantry led Birney's division. Considerable opposition was encountered, say the reports of these regiments; but after some skirmishing, Berdan managed to surround Best's command, and captured nearly the entire force.

Why Birney advanced through the woods is not readily understood; for there was a good road close by his position, leading to the Furnace, by using which many hours could have been saved.

From the prisoners of the Twenty-third Georgia, and some others intercepted, it was clearly ascertained, by two P.M., that Jackson was moving towards our right flank, with, as the prisoners stated, some forty thousand men.

These facts Sickles also reported to Hooker, requesting Pleasonton's cavalry, and his own third division, to co-operate in a flank attack, which he seems to have assumed he could make on Jackson. Hooker ordered Whipple up into supporting distance to Birney, with instructions to connect the latter with Slocum; and directed Williams (Slocum's right division) to cover the left of the advancing column, and if necessary attack the enemy there. Howard received instructions from Capt. Moore, who had been announced in general orders as on Hooker's staff, to cover Birney's right; and he detached his reserve brigade, the best and largest in the Eleventh Corps, commanded by Barlow, and led it out in person to its position.

Hooker subsequently denied having sent Capt. Moore to Howard, alleging the order to have emanated from Sickles; but, as Capt. Moore was on Hooker's staff, Howard certainly could do no less than he did, supposing the order to be by authority from headquarters.

Sickles now imagined that every thing promised the most brilliant success. He was preparing to make his attack, as he supposed, — to judge, at least, from what he says, — on Jackson's flank. "McLaws's opposition had all but ceased," says he; "and it was evident that in a few moments five or six regiments would be cut off, and fall into our hands."

But Sickles had been deceived by a simple rear-guard of the enemy; while Jackson, by a long circuit, was not only far beyond his reach, but in position to crush Howard, and cut off Sickles from communication with the rest of the army.

Pleasonton, whom Hooker had sent out to Sickles's aid, held his three regiments and Martin's horse-battery, in the clearing at Scott's Run, being unable to operate to any advantage on the ground occupied by Birney. Three or four other Third-Corps batteries were also here for a similar reason.

When Sickles's attack, leading to the capture of the Twenty-third Georgia, was made, Col. Brown's battalion of Confederate artillery happened to be within reach, and was speedily ordered up by Jackson, and placed on a cleared eminence south of the railroad cutting. Here, gathering a few detached companies in support, he opened smartly upon Sickles. The latter, bearing in mind his orders impressing caution in his advance, was for the moment checked, long enough, at all events, to enable Jackson's trains to get out of reach by the lower road.

Birney had barely reached the Furnace when Brown's fire became quite annoying. He accordingly placed Livingstone's, and afterwards Randolph's, batteries in position, and spent some time in silencing the Confederate guns; after accomplishing which, he threw forward his skirmishers, and occupied Welford's house, while Graham, with four regiments, got possession of the railroad cutting.

By this time Jackson's troops had passed a couple of miles beyond the Furnace; but on hearing of Sickles's attack, and the capture of an entire regiment, Archer, who commanded the rear brigade, promptly retraced his steps with his own and Thomas's brigades, and supported Brown's excellent work. So soon as the trains had got well along, these two brigades rejoined their command; and their work as rear-guard was undertaken by Posey, and subsequently by Wright, whom Anderson ordered out, and threw across his own left flank to engage the attention of Sickles's column.

Jackson's divisions were well out of reach, a half-dozen miles from Sickles, before this officer was ready for an advance in force. Jackson had marched on, or parallel to, the Brock road. When he reached the Orange plank road, he was shown an eminence from which he could observe the position of the Union lines. Riding up alone, so as not to attract attention, after — as Cooke affirms — driving the Federal cavalry from the spot, he examined our position carefully; and, seeing that he was not yet abreast of our flank on this road, he ordered his troops farther along the Brock road to the old turnpike.

But he sent Fitz Hugh Lee's cavalry, supported by Paxton, along the plank road, to hold it in case his designs were prematurely discovered and met.

By four P.M. he had reached the right and rear of the Union line; while Hooker complacently viewed the situation from his comfortable headquarters at the Chancellor house, apparently in a semi-torpid state, retaining just enough activity to inititate manœuvres, which, under the circumstances, were the most unfortunate possible.

For not only had he robbed his right corps of Barlow's brigade, the only general reserve of the "key of his position," as himself has called it, and despatched Birney two miles into the woods, supported by Whipple, and protected on the left by Williams; but about five P.M. he ordered Geary from his position on Slocum's left, to move forward, and make an attack down the plank road. This order Geary carried out in person with several regiments. He had a smart skirmish with the enemy, and was considerably advanced, when, about sundown, he was suddenly ordered to return to his position.

Hooker's right flank, of less than ten thousand men, was thus isolated from the rest of the army, with no supports within two miles.

And yet the full evidence of Jackson's whereabouts was before him. There had been a constant feeling of the Union lines (by Stuart's cavalry and some infantry skirmishers) all day, gradually working from east to west. This fact was noticed by many officers, and is particularly referred to by Pleasonton, Warren, and Howard. Jackson's columns and trains had been strongly reconnoitred, their force estimated, and their direction noted. The question as to what might be the objective of such a movement, had been the main topic of discussion during the day throughout the right of the army.

At noon a cavalry picket on the plank road was driven in, and gave notice of the passing of a heavy column a mile beyond our lines.   About 3.30 P.M. the leading divisions of Jackson's corps, arriving on the old turnpike, sent a party forward to feel our lines, and a ten-minutes' skirmish resulted, when the Confederate party withdrew. There had been a number of minor attacks on our outlying pickets, some of them occurring when Gen. Howard was present.   All these facts were successively reported to headquarters.

About the same time two men, sent out as spies, came in, and reported the enemy crossing the plank road on our right, in heavy columns.   These men were despatched by Howard to Hooker, with instructions to the officer accompanying them to see that Hooker promptly received their information.   On the other hand, a half-hour before Jackson's attack came, Howard sent a couple of companies of cavalry out the plank road to reconnoitre.   These men, from negligence or cowardice, failed to go far enough to ascertain the presence of Jackson, and returned and reported all quiet.   This report was, however, not forwarded to Hooker.

There was not an officer or man in the Eleventh Corps that afternoon who did not discuss the possibility of an attack in force on our right, and wonder how the small body thrown across the road on the extreme flank could meet it.   And yet familiar with all the facts related, for that they were reported to him there is too much cumulative evidence to doubt, and having inspected the line so that he was conversant with its situation, Hooker allowed the key of his position to depend upon a half-brigade and two guns, facing the enemy, while the balance of the wing, absolutely in the air, turned its back upon the general whose attack was never equalled for its terrible momentum during our war, or excelled in any, and whose crushing blows had caused the brave old Army of the Potomac more than once to stagger.

Moreover, the " key of the position " was confided to a corps which was not properly part of the Army of the Potomac, and untried as yet. For not only had the Eleventh Corps, as a corps, seen no active service, but the most of its regiments were made up of raw troops, and the elements of which the corps was composed were to a degree incongruous. Of itself this fact should have caused Hooker to devote serious attention to his right flank.

XIII.

HOOKER'S THEORIES AND CHANCES.

HOOKER and Sickles have both stated that the plan of the former was to allow this movement of Jackson's to develop itself: if it was a retreat, to attack the column at the proper time; if a tactical flank movement, to allow it to be completed, and then thrust himself between the two wings of Lee's army, and beat them in detail. This admirable generalization lacked the necessary concomitant of intelligent and speedy execution.

Now, Hooker had his choice between two theories of this movement of Jackson. It was a retreat from his front, either because Lee deemed himself compromised, or for the purpose of making new strategic combinations; or it was the massing of troops for a flank attack. It could mean nothing else. Let us, then, do Hooker all the justice the situation will allow.

All that had occurred during the day was fairly explainable on the former hypothesis. If Jackson was passing towards Culpeper, he would naturally send flanking parties out every road leading from the one his own columns were pursuing, towards our lines, for strictly defensive purposes. The several attacks of the day might have thus occurred. This assumption was quite justifiable.

And this was the theory of Howard. He knew that Hooker had all the information obtained along the entire line, from prisoners and scouts. He naturally concluded, that if there was any reasonable supposition that an attack from the west was intended, Hooker would in some way have notified him. But, far from doing this, Hooker had inspected and approved his position, and had ordered Howard's reserve away. To be sure, early in the morning, Hooker had told him to guard against an attack on the right: but since then circumstances had absolutely changed; Barlow had been taken from him, and he conjectured that the danger of attack had passed. How could he assume otherwise?

Had he suspected an attack down the pike, had he received half an hour's warning, he could, and naturally would, assuming the responsibility of a corps commander, have changed front to rear so as to occupy with his corps the line along the east side of the Dowdall's clearing, which he had already intrenched, and where he had his reserve artillery. He did not do so; and it is more easy to say that he was to blame, than to show good cause for the stigma cast upon him for the result of this day.

However much Hooker's after-wit may have prompted him to deny it, his despatch of 4.10 P.M., to Sedgwick, shows conclusively that he himself had adopted this theory of a retreat. "We know that the enemy is flying," says he, "trying to save his trains. Two of Sickles's divisions are among them."

And it is kinder to Hooker's memory to assume that he did not apprehend a flank attack on this evening. If he did, his neglect of his position was criminal. Let us glance at the map.

We know how the Eleventh Corps lay, its reserve removed, with which it might have protected a change of front, should this become necessary, and itself facing southerly. What was on its left, to move up to its support in case of an attack down the pike? Absolutely not a regiment between Dowdall's and Chancellorsville, and near the latter place only one division available. This was Berry's, still luckily massed in the open north of headquarters. And to Sickles's very deliberate movement alone is due the fact that Berry was still there when the attack on Howard burst; for Sickles had bespoken Berry's division in support of his own advance just at this juncture.

Birney, who was the prop of Howard's immediate left, had been advanced nearly two miles through the thickets to the south to attack an imaginary enemy. Whipple had followed him. Of Slocum's corps, Williams had been sent out "two or three miles," to sweep the ground in his front, and Geary despatched down the plank road "for the purpose of cutting off the train of the enemy, who was supposed to be in retreat towards Gordonsville." To oppose the attack of a column of not far from twenty-five thousand men, there was thus left a brigade front of four small regiments, and the flank of a corps of eight thousand men more, without reserves, and with no available force whatever for its support, should it be overwhelmed.

Is any criticism needed upon this situation? And who should be responsible for it?

In a defensive battle it is all-important that the general in command should hold his troops well in hand, especially when the movements of the enemy can be concealed by the *terrain.* The enemy is allowed his choice of massing for an attack on any given point: so that the ability to concentrate reserve troops on any threatened point is an indispensable element of safety. It may be assumed that Hooker was, at the moment of Jackson's attack, actually taking the offensive. But on this hypothesis, the feebleness of his advance is still more worthy of criticism. For Jackson was first attacked by Sickles as early as nine A.M.; and it was six P.M. before the latter was ready to move upon the enemy in force. Such tardiness as this could never win a battle.

While all this had been transpiring on the right, Lee, to keep his opponent busy, and prevent his sending re-enforcements to the flank Jackson was thus threatening, had been continually tapping at the lines in his front. But, owing to the small force left with him, he confined this work to Hooker's centre, where he rightly divined his headquarters to be. About seven A.M. the clearing at Chancellorsville was shelled by some of Anderson's batteries, obliging the trains there parked to go to the rear into the woods.

Hancock states that the enemy frequently opened with artillery, and made infantry assaults on his advanced line of rifle-pits, but was always handsomely repulsed. "During the sharp contests of that day, the enemy was never able to reach my principal line of battle, so stoutly and successfully did Col. Miles (who commanded the advanced line) contest the ground."

Col. Miles says his line was constantly engaged skirmishing with the enemy during the day. At about three P.M. the Confederates massed troops in two columns, one on each side the road, flanked by a line some eight hundred yards long, in the woods. An impetuous charge was made to within twenty yards of the abattis, but it was baffled by our sturdy front.

Sickles, then still in reserve, had made a reconnoissance early on Saturday, in Hancock's front, with the Eleventh Massachusetts and Twenty-sixth Pennsylvania Volunteers, covered by some sharpshooters; had driven in the enemy's pickets, and found him, to all appearances, in force. This was Anderson's line.

The Twelfth Corps had also made a reconnoissance down the plank road later in the day, but with no immediate results.

All that was accomplished was a mere feeling of the other's lines by either force. Hooker vainly endeavored to ascertain Lee's strength at various places in his front. Lee, to good purpose, strove to amuse Hooker by his bustle and stir, to deceive him as to the weakness of his force, and to gain time.

During the afternoon of Saturday, Hooker had a rare chance of redeeming his error made, the day before, in withdrawing from the open country to the Wilderness, and of dealing a fatal blow to his antagonist. He knew that Jackson, with twenty-five thousand men, was struggling through difficult roads towards his right. Whatever his object, the division of Lee's forces was a fact. He knew that there could be left in his front not more than an equal number. It was actually less than eighteen thousand men; but Hooker, with his knowledge of Lee's strength, could not estimate it at more than twenty-five thousand by any calculation he could make. Himself had over seventy thousand men in line, and ready to mass on any given point. He ought to have known that Lee was too astute a tactician seriously to attack him in front, while Jackson was manœuvring to gain his right. And all Lee's conduct during the day was palpable evidence that he was seeking to gain time.

However much Hooker may have believed that Jackson was retreating, he was bound to guard against the possibility of an attack, knowing as he did Jackson's whereabouts and habit of rapid mystery. Had he thrown the entire Eleventh Corps *en potence* to his main line, as above indicated, to arrest or retard an attack if made; had he drawn troops from Meade on the extreme left, where half an hour's reconnoitring would have shown that nothing was in his front, and from Couch's reserves in the centre; had he thrown heavy columns out where Birney was, to prevent the re-union of Jackson and Lee, and to make a determined attack upon the latter's left while Hancock pressed him in front, — half the vigor displayed in the early days of this movement would have crushed the Army of Northern Virginia beyond recovery for this campaign. Lee's only salvation would have lain in instant withdrawal from our front, and a retreat towards Gordonsville to re-unite with his lieutenant.

However he might have disposed his forces for an attack on Saturday afternoon, he could have committed no mistake as great as the half-way measures which have been narrated. And if the heavy fighting of Sunday had been done the day before with any thing like the dispositions suggested, it could have scarcely failed of brilliant success for the Army of the Potomac.

But six o'clock came: Hooker still lay listlessly awaiting an attack, with his forces disjointedly lodged, and with no common purpose of action; and Jackson had gathered for his mighty blow.

It is but fair to give weight to every circumstance which shall moderate the censure attributable to Hooker for his defeat in this campaign. Early in the morning, after his inspection of the lines on the right, which was made with thoroughness, and after receipt of the first news of the movement of troops across our front, Hooker issued the following circular : —

HEADQUARTERS ARMY OF THE POTOMAC,
CHANCELLORSVILLE, VA., May 2, 1863, 9.30 A.M.

MAJOR-GEN. SLOCUM AND MAJOR-GEN. HOWARD.

I am directed by the major-general commanding to say that the disposition you have made of your corps has been with a view to a front attack by the enemy. If he should throw himself upon your flank, he wishes you to examine the ground, and determine upon the positions you will take in that event, in order that you may be prepared for him in whatever direction he advances. He suggests that you have heavy reserves well in hand to meet this contingency. The right of your line does not appear to be strong enough. No artificial defences worth naming have been thrown up; and there appears to be a scarcity of troops at that point, and not, in the general's opinion, as favorably posted as might be.

We have good reason to suppose that the enemy is moving to our right. Please advance your pickets for purposes of observation as far as may be, in order to obtain timely information of their approach.

James H. Van Alen,

Brigadier-General and Aide-de-Camp.

Although addressed to Slocum as well as Howard, this order scarcely applied with much force to the former, who occupied the right centre of the army, with Birney lying between him and the Eleventh Corps. Howard carried out his part of these instructions as well as circumstances allowed. He posted Barlow's brigade, his largest and best, on the Buschbeck line, in position for a general reserve for the corps, and took advantage of the ground in a manner calculated to strengthen his flank, and to enable it to cover a change of front if necessary; he placed his reserve artillery on the right of the rifle-pits running across the road at Dowdall's; he located several regiments on Dowdall's clearing so as to wheel to the west or south as might be required; Major Hoffman was set to work, and spent the entire day locating and supervising the construction of field-works; and generally, Howard disposed the forces under his command after a fashion calculated to oppose a stubborn resistance to attacks down the pike, should they be made.

Later on in the day, we have seen how Hooker's aide, Capt. Moore, ordered this brigade of Barlow's away from its all-important position. We have seen Hooker's dispositions of the Third and Twelfth Corps. We have seen Hooker's 4.10 P.M. order to Sedgwick. No room is left to doubt that Hooker's opinion, if he had any, underwent a change after issuing these instructions, and that he gave up the idea of an attack upon the right. His dispositions certainly resulted in convincing Howard that he had done so.

But suppose Hooker still remained of the same opinion during the afternoon, was the issue of this circular in the morning enough? If he supposed it probable that the enemy would strike our right, was it not the duty of the commanding general, at least to *see* that the threatened flank was properly protected, — that the above order was carried out as he intended it should be? No attack sufficient to engross his attention had been made, or was particularly threatened elsewhere; and a ten-minutes' gallop would bring him from headquarters to the questionable position. He had some excellent staff-officers — Gen. Warren among others — who could have done this duty; but there is no evidence of any one having been sent. Gen. Howard, in fact, states that no inspection by, or by the order of, Gen. Hooker was made during the day, after the one in the early morning.

It may be alleged that Hooker had desired to draw in the extended right the evening before, and had yielded only to the claim that that position could be held against any attack coming from the front. This is true. But when half his enemy's forces, after this disposition was made, are moved to and massed on his right, and have actually placed themselves where they can take his line in reverse, is it still fair to urge this plea? Hooker claims that his "instructions were utterly and criminally disregarded." But inasmuch as common-sense, not to quote military routine, must hold him accountable for the removal of Barlow (for how can a general shelter himself from the consequences of the acts of his subordinates, when these acts are in pursuance of orders received from his own aide-de-camp?), and himself acknowledges the disposition made of Sickles and Slocum, can the facts be fairly said to sustain the charge? There was, moreover, so much bitterness exhibited after this campaign, that, had the facts in the slenderest degree warranted such action, formal charges would assuredly have been brought against Howard and his division commanders, on the demand alike of the commander-in-chief and a disappointed public.

XIV.

POSITION OF THE ELEVENTH CORPS.

GEN. HOWARD states that he located his command, both with reference to an attack from the south, and from the west along the old turnpike and the plank road. The whole corps lies on a ridge along which runs the turnpike, and which is the watershed of the small tributaries of the Rappahannock and Mattapony Rivers. This ridge is terminated on the right by some high and easily-defended ground near Talley's.

Gen. Devens, with the first division, holds the extreme right. He has less than four thousand men under his command. Von Gilsa's brigade has, until this morning, been half a mile farther out the pike, and across the road; but on receipt of Hooker's 9.30 order has been withdrawn, and now lies with two regiments astride and north of the pike, some distance beyond Talley's, the rest skirting the south of it. His right regiment leans upon that portion of the Brock road which is the prolongation of the eastern branch, and which, after crossing the plank road and pike, bears north-westerly, and loses itself in the woods where formerly was an old mill. McLean's brigade prolongs von Gilsa's line towards Schurz. Dieckman's battery has two pieces trained westerly down the pike, and four on Devens's left, covering, near Talley's Hill, the approaches from the plank road. Devens has the Twenty-fifth and Seventy-fifth Ohio Volunteers as a reserve, near the pike.

Schurz's (third) division continues this line on the edge of the woods to Dowdall's. His front hugs the eastern side of the clearing between the pike and the plank road, thence along the latter to the fork. Schimmelpfennig's brigade is on the right, adjoining Devens; Krzyzanowski's on the left. Three regiments of the former are on the line, and two in reserve: the latter has two regiments on the line, and two in reserve. On Schurz's right wing, the troops are shut in between thick woods and their rifle-pits, with no room whatever to manœuvre or deploy. This condition likewise applies to many of the regiments in Devens's line. The pike is the means of inter-communication, running back of the woods in their rear. Dilger's battery is placed near Dowdall's, at the intersection of the roads.

Steinwehr considers himself the reserve division. He is more or less massed near Dowdall's. Buschbeck's brigade is in the clearing south of the road, but has made a line of rifle-pits across the road, facing west, at the edge of the open ground. Two regiments are deployed, and two are in reserve. His other brigade, Barlow's, has been sent out nearly two miles, to protect Birney's right, leaving no general reserve whatever for the corps. Wiederich's battery is on Steinwehr's right and left, trained south.

Three batteries are in reserve on the line of Busch-beck's rifle-pits running north and south. Barlow had been, as above stated, massed as a general reserve of the corps on Buschbeck's right, — the only reserve the corps could boast, and a most necessary one.

Two companies, and some cavalry and artillery, have been sent to the point where the Ely's Ford road crosses Hunting Creek.

Devens states that his pickets were kept out a proper distance, and that he had constant scouting-parties moving beyond them. In his report he recapitulates the various attacks made during the day. Shortly after noon, cavalry attacked his skirmishers, but drew off. This was Stuart protecting Jackson's flank, and feeling for our lines. Then two men, sent out from Schimmelpfennig's front, came in through his, and were despatched to Hooker with their report that the enemy was in great force on our flank. Later, Lieut. Davis, of Devens's staff, with a cavalry scout, was fired upon by Confederate horse. Then von Gilsa's skirmishers were attacked by infantry, — again Stuart seeking to ascertain our position : after which the pickets were pushed farther out. Cavalry was afterwards sent out, and returned with information that some Confederate troopers, and part of a battery, were in the woods on our right.

But all this seems to have been explained as a retreat. "The unvarying report was, that the enemy is crossing the plank road, and moving towards Culpeper."

The ground about Dowdall's is a clearing of undulating fields, closed on three sides, and open to the west. As you stand east of the fork of the roads, you can see a considerable distance down the plank road, leading to Orange Court House. The pike bears off to the right, and runs up hill for half a mile, to the eminence at Talley's.

The dispositions recited were substantially the same as those made when the corps arrived here on Thursday. They were, early Saturday morning, inspected by Hooker in person, and pronounced satisfactory. As he rode along the line with Howard, and with each division commander in succession, he was greeted with the greatest enthusiasm. His exclamation to Howard, several times repeated, as he examined the position, — his mind full of the idea of a front attack, but failing to seize the danger of the two roads from the west, — was: "How strong! How strong!"

An hour or two later, having ascertained the Confederate movement across our front, he had sent his circular to Howard and Slocum. Later still, as if certain that the enemy was on the retreat, he depleted Howard's line by the withdrawal of Barlow, and made dispositions which created the gap of nigh two miles on Howard's left.

Howard, during the day, frequently inspected the line, and all dispositions were approved by him.

And, when Barlow was ordered out to the front, both Howard and Steinwehr accompanied him. They returned to Dowdall's Tavern just as Jackson launched his columns upon the Eleventh Corps.

XV.

THE SITUATION AT SIX O'CLOCK.

IT is now six o'clock of Saturday, May 2, 1863, a lovely spring evening. The Eleventh Corps lies quietly in position. Supper-time is at hand. Arms are stacked on the line; and the men, some with accoutrements hung upon the stacks, some wearing their cartridge-boxes, are mostly at the fires cooking their rations, careless of the future, in the highest spirits and most vigorous condition. Despite the general talk during the entire afternoon, among officers and rank and file alike, of a possible attack down the pike, all but a few are happily unsuspicious of the thunder-cloud gathering on their flank. There is a general feeling that it is too late to get up much of a fight to-day.

The breastworks are not very substantial. They are hastily run up out of rails from the fences, logs from barns in the vicinity, and newly felled trees. The ditch skirting the road has been deepened for this temporary purpose. Abattis, to a fair extent, has been laid in front. But the whole position faces to the south, and is good for naught else.

Nor were our men in those days as clever with the

spade as we afterwards became. This is clearly shown in the defences.

There is some carelessness apparent. Ambulances are close by the line. Ammunition-wagons and the train of pack-mules are mixed up with the regiments. Even a drove of beeves is herded in the open close by. All these properly belong well to the rear. Officers' servants and camp-gear are spread abroad in the vicinity of each command, rather more comfortably ensconced than the immediate presence of the enemy may warrant.

The ground in the vicinity is largely clearing. But dense woods cover the approaches, except in some few directions southerly. Down the roads no great distance can be seen ; perhaps a short mile on the plank road, not many hundred yards on the turnpike.

Little Wilderness Church, in the rear of the position, looks deserted and out of place. Little did its worshippers on last sabbath day imagine what a conflict would rage about its walls before they again could meet within its peaceful precincts.

There may be some absence of vigilance on the part of the pickets and scouts; though it is not traceable in the reports, nor do any of the officers concerned remember such. But the advanced line is not intrenched as Miles's line in front of Hancock has been. Less care, rather than more carelessness, is all that can be observed on this score.

Meanwhile Jackson has ranged his corps, with the utmost precaution and secrecy, in three lines, at right angles to the pike, and extending about a mile on either side.

All orders are given in a low tone. Cheering as " Old Jack " passes along is expressly prohibited.

Rodes, commanding D. H. Hill's division, leads, with Iverson's and Rodes's brigades to the left of the road, and Doles's and Colquitt's to the right. Rodes's orders to his brigades are to push on steadily, to let nothing delay or retard them. Should the resistance at Talley's Hill, which Rodes expects, render necessary the use of artillery, the line is to check its advance until this eminence is carried. But to press on, and let no obstacle stand in the way, is the watchword.

Two hundred yards in rear of the first line, Colston, commanding Trimble's division, ranges his brigades, Nichols and Jones on the left, and Colston on the right of the road; Ramseur in support.

A. P. Hill's division is not yet all up; but, as part reaches the line, it is formed in support of Colston, the balance following in column on the pike.

The second and third lines are ordered to re-enforce the first as occasion requires.

Two pieces of Stuart's horse-artillery accompany the first line on the pike.

The regiments in the centre of the line appear to have been formed in columns with intervals, each brigade advancing in line of columns by regiment. The troops are not preceded by any skirmishers. The line on the wings is probably not so much massed. It is subsequently testified by many in the Eleventh Corps, that the centre of the line appears to advance *en échiquier*, the front companies of each line of columns firing while the rear columns are advancing through the intervals.

The march through the woods up to Dowdall's clearing has not disturbed the lines so materially as to prevent the general execution of such a manœuvre.

But the Confederate reports show that the regiments were all in line and not in column. The appearance of columns was due to the fact that the second and third lines, under Colston and A. P. Hill, were already pressing up close in the rear of the first under Rodes, thus making a mass nine deep. The intervals between regiments were accidental, occasioned by the swaying of the line to and fro as it forced its way through the underbrush.

It is perhaps no more than fair to say that whatever laxity was apparent at this hour in the Eleventh Corps was by no means incompatible with a readiness to give a good account of itself if an attack should be made upon its front.

XVI.

JACKSON'S ATTACK.

SUCH is the situation at six P.M. Now Jackson gives
the order to advance; and a heavy column of twenty-
two thousand men, the best infantry in existence, as
tough, hardy, and full of *élan*, as they are ill-fed, ill-
clothed, and ill-looking, descends upon the Eleventh
Corps, whose only ready force is four regiments, the section of a battery, and a weak line of pickets.

The game, in which these woods still abound, startled
at the unusual visitors, fly in the advance of Jackson's
line towards and across the Dowdall clearing, and many a
mouth waters, as fur and feather in tempting variety rush
past; while several head of deer speedily clear the dangerous ground, before the bead of willing rifles can be
drawn upon them.

This sudden appearance of game causes as much jollity
as wonder. All are far from imagining its cause.

The next sound is that of bugles giving the command,
and enabling the advancing troops to preserve some kind
of alignment. At this the wary prick up their ears.
Surprise stares on every face. Immediately follows a
crash of musketry as Rodes sweeps away our skirmish

line as it were a cobweb. Then comes the long and
heavy roll of veteran infantry fire, as he falls upon Devens's line.

The resistance which this division can make is as nothing against the weighty assault of a line moving by battalions in mass. Many of the regiments do their duty
well. Some barely fire a shot. This is frankly acknowledged in many of the reports. What can be expected of
new troops, taken by surprise, and attacked in front, flank,
and rear, at once? Devens is wounded, but remains in
the saddle, nor turns over the command to McLean until
he has reached the Buschbeck line. He has lost one-
quarter of his four thousand men, and nearly all his superior officers, in a brief ten minutes.

Schurz's division is roused by the heavy firing on the
right, in which even inexperienced ears detect something
more than a mere repetition of the picket-fight of three
hours gone. Its commanding officers are at once alert.
Regimental field and staff are in the saddle, and the men
behind the stacks, leaving canteens, haversacks, cups with
the steaming evening coffee, and rations at the fires.
Arms are taken. Regiments are confusedly marched and
counter-marched into the most available positions, to meet
an emergency which some one should have anticipated
and provided for. The absence of Barlow is now fatal.

On comes Jackson, pursuing the wreck of the First
division. Some of Schurz's regiments break before Devens has passed to the rear. Others stand firm until the
victorious Confederates are upon them with their yell of
triumph, then steadily fall back, turning and firing at

intervals; but nowhere a line which can for more than a brief space retard such an onset.

Down the road towards Chancellorsville, through the woods, up every side road and forest path, pours a stream of fugitives. Ambulances and oxen, pack-mules and ammunition-wagons, officers' spare horses mounted by runaway negro servants, every species of the *impedimenta* of camp-life, commissary sergeants on all-too-slow mules, teamsters on still-harnessed team-horses, quartermasters whose duties are not at the front, riderless steeds, clerks with armfuls of official papers, non-combatants of all kinds, mixed with frighted soldiers whom no sense of honor can arrest, strive to find shelter from the murderous fire.

No organization is left in the Eleventh Corps but one brigade of Steinwehr's division. Buschbeck has been speedily formed by a change of front, before Devens and Schurz have left the field, in the line of intrenchments built across the road at Dowdall's at the edge of the clearing. No sooner in place than a scattering fire by the men is opened upon friends and foes alike. Dilger's battery trains some of its guns down the road. The reserve artillery is already in position at the north of this line, and uses spherical case with rapidity. Howard and his staff are in the thickest of the fray, endeavoring to stem the tide. As well oppose resistance to an avalanche.

Buschbeck's line stubbornly holds on. An occasional squad, still clinging to the colors of its regiment, joins itself to him, ashamed of falling thus disgracefully to the rear. Officers make frantic exertions to rally their men;

useless effort. In little less than half an hour this last
stand has been swept away, and the Eleventh Corps is in
confused retreat down the pike towards headquarters, or
in whatever direction affords an outlet from the remorse-
less hail.

The general confusion which reigned can scarcely be
more accurately described than by detailing the experience of a single regiment. The One Hundred and Nine-
teenth New York Volunteers was in Schurz's division. It
was commanded by an officer of German birth, but long
since an American citizen. No more gallant, intelligent
man wore uniform, or one better fitted for a pattern soldier. Well read in military matters, he had never yet
been under fire, and was nervously anxious to win his
spurs. The regiment was a good one; but only three or
four officers, and a small percentage of enlisted men, had
seen service.

This regiment faced south on the pike just west of the
fork in the roads. Under arms in an instant, when the
firing was heard on the right, it was soon ordered by one
of Schurz's aides to throw itself across the fork, and hold
it at all hazards. But the suddenness of the attack had
momentarily robbed Col. Peissner of his steadiness, for
he was a good drill-master. Instead of facing to the right,
counter-marching, filing to the left across the road, and
coming to a front, — the simplest if longest movement
being the best in times of such excitement, — he faced to
the left because his left was nearest to the fork, filed to
the left, and then, instead of coming on the left by file
into line, he moved astride the roads, and ordered "Front!"

This brought the regiment in line *with its back to the enemy*. The men instinctively came each to an about-face, and the file closers broke through to the now rear. There was no time to correct the error. The regiment, which would have fought well under proper circumstances, from the start lost confidence in its officers and itself. Still it held its ground until it had burned almost twenty rounds, and until the Confederate line was within fifty yards in its face, and had quite outflanked it. Then the raking volleys of such a front as Jackson was wont to present, and, more than all, the fire of Buschbeck's brigade in its immediate rear, broke it; and it melted away, leaving only a platoon's strength around the colors, to continue for a brief space the struggle behind the Buschbeck line, while the rest fled down the road, or through the woods away from the deadly fire. This regiment lost its entire color-guard, and nearly one-half of its complement killed or wounded.

There is much discrepancy as to the time during which the Eleventh Corps made resistance to Jackson's advance. All reliable authorities put the time of the attack as six P.M. When the last gun was fired at the Buschbeck rifle-pits, it was dusk, at that season about quarter past seven. It seems reasonably settled, therefore, that the corps retarded the Confederate advance over about a mile of ground for exceeding an hour. How much more can be expected of ten thousand raw troops telescoped by twenty-five thousand veterans?

Rodes, now quite mixed with Colston's line, still pressed on, and between Hooker's headquarters and his elated foe there was scarce an organized regiment. Hooker's fatal inability to grasp the situation, and his ordering an advance of all troops on Howard's left as far as the Second Corps, had made him almost defenceless. The troops which should have been available to stem this adverse tide were blindly groping in the woods, two miles in front, — in pursuit of Jackson.

One cannot but wonder just where Sickles expected to find Jackson. There can be little doubt that he did think he was about to strike Jackson's flank. His testimony before the Committee on the Conduct of the War constantly refers to this belief; and he says that he "was about to open his attack in full force," was holding Pleasonton's cavalry in hand, desiring to lead the attack with his infantry, when the news of the disaster to the Eleventh Corps was brought to him; and that every thing seemed to indicate the most brilliant success from thus throwing himself upon Jackson's flank and rear. He refers to McLaws being in his front, but this is an error. McLaws was on Lee's right flank, three miles away. It was with Archer of Jackson's corps, and with Posey and Wright of Anderson's division, that he had to do.

The reports are by no means clear as to the details of these movements. Birney states in his testimony before the Committee on the Conduct of the War, that he found that he and Barlow "had got into the midst of the rebel army, the supports on the left not having come up." He therefore formed his command into a huge square, with the artillery in the centre, holding the road over which Jackson had passed. "The fire upon his left flank from musketry was galling." This came from Anderson's brigades.

Hayman, Graham and Ward were pushed out along the road, and "found the enemy in some force on three sides." This apparently shows that Birney, — who had the immediate command of the troops in front, — was quite uncertain of what was before him, or just what he was expected to do.

This much is, however, clear: Jackson's small rearguard had succeeded in holding the road which he had traversed, at some point near Welford's; and here this force remained until Jackson was well along towards the plank road. Then Anderson in his turn made a diversion on the other side of Birney, which kept the latter busy for at least a couple of hours.

Sickles's orders were to advance cautiously. This was Hooker's doing. Hence exception cannot fairly be taken to either Birney's or Sickles's conduct for lack of energy. But the latter must have singularly underrated Jackson's methods, if he thought he could strike him at a given point, so many hours after his passage. For Jackson was first observed near the Furnace about eight A.M., and Sickles was just getting ready to attack him in this same place at six P.M.

The errors of judgment on this entire day can scarcely be attributed to any one but the general commanding. He was the one to whom all reports were sent. He had knowledge of every thing transpiring. He it was who was responsible for some sensible interpretation of the information brought him, and for corresponding action in the premises.

So much for Sickles's advance. It could not well have been more ill-timed and useless. But his gallant work of the coming night and morrow, when Hooker left him almost alone to resist the fierce assaults of our victorious and elated foe, was ample compensation for his subordinate share in the triviality and fatal issue of Saturday's manœuvring. Nor can blame fall upon him in as full measure as upon Hooker; although he seems illy to have construed what was transpiring in his front, and what he reported may have seriously misled his chief.

Perhaps no officers, during our Civil War, were placed in a more lamentably awkward position than Devens, and in a less degree Schurz, on this occasion. Having been fully convinced by the events of the afternoon that an attack down the pike was highly probable, having carefully reported all these events to his immediate commander, Devens was left without inspection, counsel, or help. He might have gone in person to Howard, but he did not dare leave his division. He might have sent messages which more urgently represented his own anxiety. But when the blow came, he did all that was possible, and remained, wounded, in command, and assisted in re-organizing some relics of his division behind the Buschbeck works.

Schurz was with Howard a good part of the day, and his opinions were expressed to that officer. To Schurz's personal bearing here, or on any other occasion, no possible exception can be taken.

XVII.

THE CONDUCT OF THE ELEVENTH CORPS.

THERE can be no attempt to gainsay that the Eleventh Corps, on this luckless Saturday, did not do its whole duty. That it was panic-stricken, and that it decamped from a field where as a corps it had not fought, is undeniable. But portions of the corps did fight, and the entire corps would doubtless have fought well under favorable circumstances. It is but fair, after casting upon the corps the aspersion of flight from before the enemy, to do it what justice is possible, and to palliate the bad conduct of the whole by bearing testimony to the good conduct of some of its parts.

It has been called a German corps. This is not quite exact. Of nearly thirteen thousand men in the corps, only forty-five hundred were Germans. But it must be admitted that so many officers high in rank were of that nationality, that the general tendency and feeling were decidedly unlike the rest of the army. Moreover, there is not wanting testimony to show that there were some who wore shoulder-straps in the corps who gave evidence of having taken up the profession of arms to make money, and not to fight.

The artillery of the corps did well. Those general officers who most severely rebuke the conduct of the corps, all say a word in favor of the service of the guns. Dilger, on the road, just at Buschbeck's line, fired with his own hands from his last gun a round of canister when the Confederates were within a dozen yards. Most of the guns had been well served, but had been sent to the rear in time to save them from capture.

The reserve artillery did its duty, nor limbered up until the Confederate line had outflanked its position, rendered it useless, and jeopardized its safety.

All the guns that were saved were put into action an hour later, and did effective service on the Fairview crest, in company with the artillery of the Third and Twelfth Corps.

At the time of the attack, which was made by Jackson without an advance of skirmishers, Devens's reserve regiments were ordered up to support von Gilsa. There appears to have been something like a stand attempted; but the left wing of the Confederate line speedily enveloped von Gilsa's front, and showed in rear of his right flank, when his regiments melted away.

Devens states in his report that a new line might have been formed on Gen. Schurz's division, if the latter had maintained his ground, but acknowledges that the falling-back of his own troops "must undoubtedly have added to the difficulties encountered by the command of that officer."

Schurz's report is very clear and good. This is partly attributable to the avalanche of abuse precipitated upon his division by the press, which called forth his detailed explanation, and an official request for permission to publish his report. There existed a general understanding that Schurz held the extreme right; and the newspapermen, to all appearance, took pleasure in holding a German responsible, in their early letters, for the origin of the panic. This error, together with the fact of his having discussed the situation during the day with Gen. Howard, and of his having remained of the opinion that an attack on our right was probable, accounts for the care exhibited in his statements. That he did harbor such fears is proved by his having, of his own motion, after the attack of three o'clock, placed the Fifty-Eighth New York, Eighty-Second Ohio, and Twenty-Sixth Wisconsin Volunteers, near Hawkins's farm, in the north part of the Dowdall clearing, and facing west. Still Schurz's report is only a careful summary of facts otherwise substantiated. He deals no more in his own opinions than a division commander has a right to do.

Schurz states that he strongly advised that the entire corps should take up the Buschbeck line, not considering the woods a reliable *point d'appui*. For they were thick enough to screen the manœuvring of the enemy, but not, as the event showed, to prevent his marching through them to the attack.

When the onset came, it was impossible quickly to change front. Schurz's regiments were all hemmed in between the rifle-pits before them and the woods in their rear. Still, more than half of the regiments of this division appear to have maintained their credit, and the testimony would tend to show that the men burned from five to thirty rounds each. But without avail. They were telescoped. Their defences were rendered useless. The enemy was on both sides of and perpendicular to them. It is an open question whether, at that time, any two divisions of the army could have changed front and made a good defence under these circumstances. Later in the war our soldiers were more habituated, particularly in the West, to fighting on either side of their breastworks. But these were raw troops. And this was not the first, nor was it the last, panic in the Army of the Potomac. But the corps had, as ill-luck willed it, nothing in its rear to repair or conceal its discomfiture.

Buschbeck's brigade had better opportunities, and acted correspondingly better. It had time to occupy the rifle-pits facing west before the enemy had completed the destruction of the first and third divisions. Buschbeck's stand covered a full half-hour. He was re-enforced by many fragments of broken regiments, holding together under such officers as had escaped utter demoralization. The troops remained behind these works until outflanked on right and left, for Jackson's front of over two miles easily enveloped any line our little force could form.

During the early part of the attack, Colquitt's brigade ran across the pickets of Devens's and Schurz's south front, which there had been no time to call in. Instead of joining in the advance, Colquitt remained to engage these latter, deeming it essential to protect Jackson's right. This was the nucleus of one of the many detached engagements of this day. Several bodies of Union troops thus isolated were captured *en masse.*

The reports of the officers concerned, as a rule, possess the merit of frankness. As an instance, Col. Hartung, of the Seventy-Fourth New York, relates that he had no opportunity to fire a shot until after he arrived behind the Buschbeck intrenchments. The facts would appear to be given in an even-handed way, in all the reports rendered.

Little remains to be said. The Eleventh Corps was panic-stricken, and did run, instead of retreating. It was a mere disorganized mass in a half-hour from the beginning of the attack, with but a few isolated regiments, and one brigade, retaining a semblance of orderliness.

But was it so much the misbehavior of the troops as the faultiness of the position they occupied?

The corps was got together again before Sunday morning, in a condition to do good service. Had it been tested, it would, in all probability, have fought well.

The loss of the corps was one-quarter of its effective.

Some time after the battle of Chancellorsville, a motion was made to break up the Eleventh Corps, and distribute its regiments among the others; but it was not done. Hooker then remarked that he would yet make that corps fight, and be proud of its name. And it subsequently did sterling service. Gen. Thomas remarked, in congratulating Hooker on his victory at Lookout Mountain, that "the bayonet-charge of Howard's troops, made up the side of a steep and difficult hill, over two hundred feet high, completely routing and driving the enemy from his barricades on its top, . . . will rank with the most distinguished feats of arms of this war." And it is asserted that this encomium was well earned, and that no portion of it need be set down to encouragement.

In their evidence before the Committee on the Conduct
of the War, Hooker and Sickles both testify that the
panic of the Eleventh Corps produced a gap in the line,
and that this was the main cause of disaster on this field.
But the fatal gap was made long before the Eleventh
Corps was attacked. It was Hooker's giddy blunder in
ordering away, two miles in their front, the entire line
from Dowdall's to Chancellorsville, that made it.

This was the gap which enabled Jackson to push his
advance to within a few hundred yards of Chancellorsville before he could be arrested. This was what made it
possible for him to join his right to Lee's left wing next
day. Had Hooker but kept his troops in hand, so as to
have moved up Birney sharply in support, to have thrown
forward Berry and Whipple if required, the Confederate
advance would, in all human probability, have been
checked at Dowdall's; Lee and Jackson would still have
been separated by a distance of two miles; and of this
perilous division excellent advantage could have yet been
taken at daylight Sunday by the Army of the Potomac.

Hooker's testimony includes the following attempt to
disembarrass himself of the onus of the faulty position of
the Eleventh Corps and its consequences: " No pickets
appear to have been thrown out; and I have reason to
suppose that no effort was made by the commander of the
corps on the right to follow up and keep himself advised
of Jackson's movements, although made in broad daylight, and with his full knowledge. In this way the Eleventh Corps was lost to me, and more than that, because
its bad conduct impaired the confidence that the corps of

the army had in one another. I observed this fact during the night, from the firing on the picket-lines, as well as from the general manner of the troops, if a gun was fired by the enemy: after that, the whole line would let off their pieces. The men seemed to be nervous; and during the coming-in of the Eleventh Corps I was fearful, at one time, that the whole army would be thrown into confusion by it. Some of my staff-officers killed half **a dozen of the men in trying to arrest their flight.**"

It is not intended, by what has been said, to exonerate Howard at the expense of Hooker. To Howard will always be imputed, and justly, a certain part of the blame; for there were, during the afternoon, enough indications of a probable attack down the pike to make a prudent corps-commander either assume the responsibility of a change of front, — as it could advantageously be made on the Buschbeck line prolonged, — or else, at least, so strongly urge the facts on his superior that no blame could cling to his own skirts. But neither can Hooker's larger share of blame be shifted off his own to Howard's shoulders. While it may be said that the latter did not exhibit the activity which the questionable aspect of affairs demanded, — for he did not personally inspect his lines after the early morning hours, — it is equally true that the commander of the army utterly neglected his right wing, though he had every circumstance relating to its danger reported to him.

XVIII.

HOOKER'S PARRY.

THE position of the Army of the Potomac is critical in the extreme. But several circumstances come to the rescue. It is almost dark. The rebel lines have become inextricably mixed. Colston, who has gradually moved up to Rodes's support, is so completely huddled together with this latter's command, that there is no organization left. Still Jackson's veterans press on, determined to crush our army beyond recovery, and drive it from United-States Ford. Stuart has in fact, at his own suggestion, got orders to move his cavalry division in that direction, and occupy the road to Ely's. A. P. Hill's division is still intact in rear of the two leading lines, now shuffled into one quite unmanageable mass, but still instinctively pushing forward.

So faulty have Hooker's dispositions been, in advancing his entire right centre without filling the gap, that the only available troops to throw into the breach, after the rapid destruction of the Eleventh Corps, are Berry's division of the old Third. These hardened soldiers are still in reserve on the clearing, north of headquarters. It is fortunate, indeed, that they are still there; for Sickles has just asked for their detail to join his own column out in the woods, and an hour ago Berry would certainly have been sent.

This division is at once thrown across the pike on the first crest below Fairview, west of Chancellorsville. The artillery of the Eleventh Corps is in part re-assembled. Capt. Best, chief of artillery of the Twelfth Corps, has already trained his guns upon the advancing Confederate columns, to protect the new line. But Berry is almost alone. Hays's brigade of the Second Corps, on his right, is his only support. The Excelsior brigade is rapidly pushed into the woods, north of the plank road; the Fourth Excelsior and the First Massachusetts south. Carr's brigade is kept in second line, one hundred and fifty yards in the rear. The men, with the instinctive pride of self-reliance, move up with the steadiness of veterans on drill, regardless of the stream of fugitives breaking through their intervals.

The flight of the Eleventh Corps has stampeded part of the Third Corps artillery. But it is re-assembled in short order, and at once thrown into service. Capt. Best manages by seven P.M. to get thirty-four guns into line on the crest, well served. Himself is omnipresent. Dimick's and Winslow's batteries under Osborn, Berry's chief of artillery, join this line on the hill, leaving a section of Dimick on the road. And such part of the *disjecta membra* of the Eleventh Corps as retains semblance of organization is gathered in support of the guns. Capt. Best has begun to fire solid shot over the heads of Berry's men into the woods beyond; and, as Gen. Lee says, the Confederate advance is checked in front of this crest by the vigorous opposition encountered.

Hurried orders are despatched to Geary to withdraw his attack, and re-occupy his breastworks. This he straightway accomplishes. Similar orders are carried to Williams. But, before the latter can retrace his steps, Jackson's columns have reached the right of his late position. Anderson also advances against him; so that Williams is obliged to move cautiously by his left, and change front when he arrives where his line had lately joined Geary's, and, being unable to take up his old post, he goes into position, and prolongs Berry, south of the pike. It is long after dark before he ascertains his bearings, and succeeds in massing his division where it is needed.

Anxious as Jackson is to press on, — "Give me one hour more of daylight, and I will have United-States Ford!" cries he, — he finds that he must re-establish order in his scattered forces before he can launch this night attack upon our newly formed but stubbornly maintained lines.

Nor is the darkness the most potent influence toward this end. Illy as Sickles's advance has resulted thus far, it is now a sovereign element in the salvation of the Army of the Potomac. His force at the Furnace, Birney, Whipple, Barlow, and Pleasonton, amounts to fifteen thousand men, and over forty guns. None of these officers are the men to stand about idle. No sooner has Sickles been persuaded by a second courier, — the first he would not credit, — that the Eleventh Corps has been destroyed, and that Jackson is in his rear, than he comprehends that now, indeed, the time has come to batter Jackson's flank. He orders his column to the right about, and moves up with all speed to the clearing, where Pleasonton has held his cavalry, near Birney's old front.

Howard, upon being attacked, had sent hurriedly for a cavalry regiment. Pleasonton, having received orders to send him one, instructed Major Huey, commanding the Eighth Pennsylvania Cavalry, to march to Dowdall's and report to Howard. Huey set out by the wood road which leads through Hazel Grove into the plank road. From the testimony of the persons chiefly concerned it would appear that, at the time this order was given by Pleasonton to Huey, there was at Hazel Grove, where the cavalry regiments were drawn up, no sign whatever of the disaster to Howard. There were no fugitives nor any confusion. Nor does the evidence show that Pleasonton ordered any charge on the enemy : it rather shows that Huey was not directed to go at urgent speed. And he must have been very deliberate in his movement, for by the time the cavalry had reached the vicinity of the plank road, Jackson had demolished the Eleventh Corps, and had advanced so far that the head of this cavalry column, marching by twos, suddenly came upon the Confederate lines. The officers in the lead at once gave the order to charge, and right gallantly did these intrepid horsemen ride down into the seething mass of exultant Confederate infantry. The shock was nobly given and home, but was, of course, in the woods and against such odds, of no great effect. Thirty men and three officers, including Major Keenan, were killed. Only one Confederate report — Iverson's — mentions this charge. Its effect was local only.

Three batteries of Whipple's division had remained in the Hazel Grove clearing while the infantry had advanced towards the Furnace. When the rout of the Eleventh Corps became clear, these eighteen guns were ordered in battery, facing about north-west, by their commander, Capt. Huntington, and kept up a heavy fire upon the woods through which Jackson was pushing his way. Pleasonton, for his part, trained Martin's horse-battery in the same direction. Other guns were later added to these, and all expended a good deal of ammunition on the enemy's lines. But there was no fighting at Hazel Grove rising to the distinction of a battle. The importance given to it by Sickles and Pleasonton is not borne out by the facts. There was no Federal loss, to speak of; nor do the Confederate reports make any comment upon this phase of the battle. They probably supposed these guns to be an extension of the line of batteries at Fairview. As such they were, without question, of no inconsiderable use.

Meanwhile Birney, sending word to Barlow that they run danger of being cut off, and detailing the Twentieth Indiana and Sixty-third Pennsylvania Volunteers as rear-guard, rejoins Sickles and Pleasonton in the clearing, and both move up to sustain his flank.

So soon as Jackson's guns gave Lee the intimation of his assault, the latter advanced upon the Union line with sufficient vigor to prevent Hooker from sending re-enforcements to his right. The attack was sharp; and a general inclination to the left was ordered, to connect with Jackson's right as the latter brought his columns nearer. "These orders were well executed, our troops advancing up to the enemy's intrenchments, while several batteries played with good effect upon his lines until prevented by increasing darkness." (*Lee.*)

McLaws reports: " My orders were to hold my position, not to engage seriously, but to press strongly so soon as it was discovered that Gen. Jackson had attacked . . . when I ordered an advance along the whole line to engage with the skirmishers, which were largely re-enforced, and to threaten, but not attack seriously; in doing which Gen. Wofford became so seriously engaged, that I directed him to withdraw, which was done in good order, his men in good spirits, after driving the enemy to their intrenchments."

The movement of Anderson towards the left made a gap of considerable distance in the Confederate line; " but the skirmishers of Gen. Semmes, the entire Tenth Georgia, were perfectly reliable, and kept the enemy to his intrenchments."

These accounts vary in no wise from those of the Union generals, who held their positions in front of both Anderson and McLaws, and kept inside their field-works.

Meade, whose line on the left of the army was not disturbed, sent Sykes's division, so soon as the Eleventh Corps rout became known to him, to the junction of the roads to Ely's and United-States Fords, to hold that point at all hazards, and form a new right flank. This was done with Sykes's accustomed energy. Nor was he reached by Jackson's line, and before morning Reynolds fell in upon his right.

XIX.

THE MIDNIGHT ATTACK.

WHEN his troops had been summarily brought to a standstill by Berry's firm ranks and the heavy artillery fire, Jackson determined to withdraw his first and second lines to Dowdall's clearing to reform, and ordered A. P. Hill forward to relieve them.

While this manœuvre, rendered extremely difficult by the nature of the woods in which the fighting had been done, but which Hooker was in no condition to interfere with, was in progress, Sickles and Pleasonton, whose position was considerably compromised, sought measures to re-establish communication with the headquarters of the army.

Sickles despatched Col. Hart, with a cavalry escort, to Hooker, bearing a detailed statement of his situation. This officer experienced no little difficulty in reaching Chancellorsville. The roads being in possession of the enemy, he was forced to make his way through the woods and ravines. But after the lapse of a number of hours he succeeded in his mission, and brought back word to hold on to the position gained. Sickles had so advised, and had, moreover, requested permission to make a night attack, to recover some guns, caissons, and Whipple's ammunition-train, which had been left in the woods in Sickles's front, and to enable him to join his right to Slocum's new line, thrown out in prolongation of Berry.

It will be observed that Sickles was now facing northerly, and that his rear had no obstacle on which to rest, so as to save him from the attack of Lee, had the latter been aware of the weakness of his position.

In view of this fact, a move was made somewhat to his right, where a crest was occupied near Hazel Grove. Here, says Pleasonton, "with the support of Gen. Sickles's corps we could have defeated the whole rebel army." It was clearly a strong position; for it is thus referred to by Stuart, after our troops had been next day withdrawn: "As the sun lifted the mist that shrouded the field, it was discovered that the ridge on the extreme right was a fine position for concentrating artillery. I immediately ordered thirty pieces to that point. . . . The effect of this fire upon the enemy's batteries was superb." Its possession by the Confederates did, in fact, notably contribute to the loss of the new lines at Chancellorsville in Sunday morning's action.

From this position, at precisely midnight, Sickles made a determined onslaught upon the Confederate right. It was clear, full moonlight, and operations could be almost as well conducted as during the daytime, in these woods.

Birney stationed Ward in the first line, and Hays in the second, one hundred yards in the rear. The regiments moved by the right of companies, with pieces uncapped, and strict orders to rely solely upon the bayonet. On the road from the Furnace north, parallel to which the columns moved, the Fortieth New York, Seventeenth Maine, and Sixty-Third Pennsylvania Volunteers pushed in, in columns of companies at full distance.

Berry had been notified to sustain this attack by a movement forward from his lines, if it should strike him as advisable.

The attack was made with consummate gallantry. Sickles states that he drove the enemy back to our original lines, enabling us for the moment to re-occupy the Eleventh Corps rifle-pits, and to re-capture several pieces of artillery, despite the fire of some twenty Confederate guns which had been massed at Dowdall's.

Thus attacked in flank, though the Confederate right had been refused at the time of Pleasonton's fight, and still remained so, Hill's line replied by a front movement of his left on Berry, without being able, however, to break the latter's line.

Slocum states that he was not aware that this advance was to be made by Sickles across his front. Imagining it to be a movement by the enemy on Williams, he ordered fire to be opened on all troops that appeared, and fears "that our losses must have been severe from our own fire." Williams, however, does not think so much damage was done, and alleges that he himself understood what the movement was, without, however, quoting the source of his information.

The Confederate reports state that this attack was met and repulsed by the Eighteenth, Twenty-eighth, and

Thirty-third North-Carolina regiments, with small difficulty or loss.

It is, however, probable that these as much underrate the vigor and effect of the attack, as Sickles may overstate it. It is not impossible that some portion of the Eleventh Corps position was actually reached by these columns. The road down which the movement was made strikes the plank road but a short distance east of the position of Buschbeck's line. This ground was not held in force by Jackson's corps at the moment, and it was not difficult for Sickles to possess himself temporarily of some portion of that position. But it must have been a momentary occupation.

Birney retired to Hazel Grove after this sally, having recovered part of Whipple's train, and one or two guns.

There can be found in the Confederate and Union reports alike, numerous statements which are not sustained by other testimony. As a sample, Gen. Lane of A. P. Hill's division states that a Lieut. Emack and four men captured an entire Pennsylvania regiment, under Lieut.-Col. Smith. The nearest approach to this is found in the capture of Col. Mathews and two hundred men of the One Hundred and Twenty-Eighth Pennsylvania, while Williams was moving by his left to regain his old ground. But it is highly probable that it required more than five men to effect the capture.

A wise rebuke of careless statements in official reports is found in the following indorsements on a report made of the operations of the One Hundred and Fourteenth Pennsylvania : —

In forwarding this report, which I do merely as a matter of duty, it is incumbent upon me to say that it is a complete romance from beginning to end. Col. Collis has had his attention called to these errors, but has refused to correct them.

CHAS. K. GRAHAM,
Brigadier General.

HEADQUARTERS FIRST DIVISION THIRD CORPS,
May 17, 1863.

This paper is forwarded with attention called to Brig.-Gen. Graham's indorsement. The officer is under arrest on charges of misbehavior before the enemy.

D. B. BIRNEY,
Brigadier General commanding Division.

XX.

STONEWALL JACKSON.

IT is probable that the wounding of Jackson at this juncture was the most effectual cause of the Confederate check on Saturday night. It occurred just after Jackson had concluded to withdraw his first and second lines to Dowdall's, there to re-form, and was making dispositions to move up A. P. Hill to relieve them. Orders had been issued to the troops not to fire unless at Union cavalry appearing in their front. Jackson, with some staff-officers and orderlies, had ridden out beyond his lines, as was his wont, to reconnoitre. On his return he was fired at by his own men, being mistaken in the gloom for a Federal scout. Endeavoring to enter at another place, a similar error was made, this time killing some of the party, and wounding Jackson in several places. He was carried to the rear. A few days after, he died of pneumonia brought on by his injury, which aggravated a cold he was suffering from at the time.

A. P. Hill was wounded somewhat later that night.

After the disabling of these two officers, Stuart was sent for, and promptly assumed command. With Col. Alexander, chief artillery officer present for duty, (Gen.

Crutchfield being wounded,) he spent the night rectifying the Confederate lines, and selecting positions for his batteries. It had been Jackson's plan to push forward at night, to secure the speediest results of his victory. But Stuart, after the attacks upon his right by Sickles and Pleasonton, and having in view the disorganized condition of his troops, thought wise to defer a general assault until daylight. Having submitted the facts to Jackson, and received word from this officer to use his own discretion in the matter, he decided to afford his troops a few hours of rest. They were accordingly halted in line, and lay upon their arms, an ample force of skirmishers thrown out in front.

No better place than this will be found in which to say a few words about the remarkable man who planned and led this movement about Hooker's flank, — a manœuvre which must have been condemned as foolhardy if unsuccessful, but whose triumph wove a final wreath to crown his dying brows.

Thomas J. Jackson entered West Point a poor boy, essentially a son of the people. He was a classmate of McClellan, Foster, Reno, Stoneman, Couch, Gibbon, and many other noted soldiers, as well those arrayed against as those serving beside him. His standing in his class was far from high; and such as he had was obtained by hard, persistent work, and not by apparent ability. He was known as a simple, honest, unaffected fellow, rough, and the reverse of social; but he commanded his companions' sincere respect by his rugged honesty, the while his uncouth bearing earned him many a jeer.

He was graduated in 1846, and went to Mexico as second lieutenant of the First United-States Artillery. He was promoted to be first lieutenant "for gallant and meritorious services at Vera Cruz." Twice mentioned in Scott's reports, and repeatedly referred to by Worth and Pillow for gallantry while with Magruder's battery, he emerged from that eventful campaign with fair fame and abundant training.

We find him shortly afterwards professor at the Virginia Military Institute of Lexington. Here he was known as a rigid Presbyterian, and a "fatalist," if it be fatalism to believe that "what will be will be," — Jackson's constant motto.

Tall, gaunt, awkward, grave, brief, and business-like in all he did, Jackson passed for odd, "queer," — insane almost, he was thought by some, — rather than a man of uncommon reserve power.

It was only when on parade, or when teaching artillery practice, that he brightened up; and then scarcely to lose his uncouth habit, but only to show by the light in his eye, and his wrapt attention in his work, where lay his happiest tendencies.

His history during the war is too well known to need to be more than briefly referred to. He was made colonel of volunteers, and sent to Harper's Ferry in May, 1861, and shortly after promoted to a brigade. He accompanied Joe Johnston in his retreat down the valley. At Bull Run, where his brigade was one of the earliest in the war to use the bayonet, he earned his *soubriquet* of "Stonewall" at the lips of Gen. Bee. But in the mouths of his soldiers his pet name was " Old Jack," and the term was a talisman which never failed to inflame the heart of every man who bore arms under his banner.

Jackson possessed that peculiar magnetism which stirs the blood of soldiers to boiling-point. Few leaders have ever equalled him in his control of troops. His men had no questions to ask when " Old Jack " led the way. They believed in him as did he in his star; and the impossible only arrested the vigor of their onset, or put a term to their arduous marches.

His campaign in the valley against Fremont and Shields requires no praise. And his movement about McClellan's flank at Mechanicsville, and his still more sterling manœuvre in Pope's campaign, need only to be called to mind.

In the field he was patient, hard-working, careless of self, and full of forethought for his men; though no one could call for and get from troops such excessive work, on the march or in action. No one could ask them to forego rations, rest, often the barest necessaries of life, and yet cheerfully yield him their utmost efforts, as could " Old Jack."

He habitually rode an old sorrel horse, leaning forward in a most unmilitary seat, and wore a sun-browned cap, dingy gray uniform, and a stock, into which he would settle his chin in a queer way, as he moved along with abstracted look. He paid little heed to camp comforts, and slept on the march, or by snatches under trees, as he might find occasion; often begging a cup of bean-coffee and a bit of hard bread from his men, as he passed them

in their bivouacs. He was too uncertain in his movements, and careless of self, for any of his military family
to be able to look after his physical welfare. In fact, a
cold occasioned by lending his cloak to one of his staff, a
night or two before Chancellorsville, was the primary
cause of the pneumonia, which, setting in upon his exhaust-
ing wounds, terminated his life.

Jackson was himself a bad disciplinarian. Nor had he
even average powers of organization. He was in the field
quite careless of the minutiæ of drill. But he had a singularly happy faculty for choosing men to do his work for
him. He was a very close calculator of all his movements. He worked out his manœuvres to the barest
mathematical chances, and insisted upon the unerring
execution of what he prescribed; and above all he believed in mystery. Of his entire command, he alone
knew what work he had cut out for his corps to do. And
this was carried so far that it is said the men were often
forbidden to ask the names of the places through which
they marched. " Mystery," said Jackson, "mystery is the
secret of success in war, as in all transactions of human
life."

Jackson was a professing member of the Presbyterian
Church, and what is known as a praying man. By this is
meant, that, while he never intentionally paraded or
obtruded upon his associates his belief in the practical and
immediate effect of prayer, he made no effort to hide his
faith or practice from the eyes of the world. In action,
while the whole man was wrought up to the culminating
pitch of enthusiasm, and while every fibre of his mind and

heart was strained towards the achievement of his purpose, his hand would often be instinctively raised up-
wards; and those who knew him best, believed this to be
a sign that his trust in the help of a Higher Power was
ever present.

Jackson was remarkable as a fighter. In this he stands
with but one or two peers. Few men in the world's history have ever got so great results from armed men as he
was able to do. But to judge rightly of his actual military strength is not so easy as to award this praise.
Unless a general has commanded large armies, it is difficult to judge of how far he may be found wanting if tried
in that balance. In the detached commands which he
enjoyed, in the Valley and elsewhere, his strategic ability
was marked: but these commands were always more or
less limited; and, unlike Lee or Johnston, Jackson did not
live long enough to rise to the command of a large army
upon an extended and independent field of operations.

In Gen. Lee, Jackson reposed an implicit faith. "He
is the only man I would follow blindfold," said Jackson.
And Lee's confidence in his lieutenant's ability to carry
out any scheme he set his hand to, was equally pronounced. Honestly, though with too much modesty, did
Lee say: "Could I have directed events, I should have
chosen, for the good of the country, to have been disabled
in your stead."

But, illy as Lee could spare Jackson, less still could the
Army of Northern Virginia spare Robert E. Lee, — the
greatest in adversity of the soldiers of our civil war.
Still, after Jackson's death, it is certain that Lee found no

one who could attempt the bold manœuvres on the field of battle, or the hazardous strategic marches, which have illumined the name of Jackson to all posterity.

It is not improbable that had Jackson lived, and risen to larger commands, he would have been found equal to the full exigencies of the situation. Whatever he was called upon to do, under limited but independent scope, seems to testify to the fact that he was far from having reached his limit. Whatever he did was thoroughly done; and he never appears to have been taxed to the term of his powers, in any operation which he undertook.

Honesty, singleness of purpose, true courage, rare ability, suffice to account for Jackson's military success. But those alone who have served under his eye know to what depths that rarer, stranger power of his has sounded them : they only can testify to the full measure of the strength of Stonewall Jackson.

XXI.

THE POSITION AT FAIRVIEW.

G EN. HOOKER'S testimony before the Committee on the Conduct of the War comprises almost every thing which has been officially put forth by him with reference to this campaign. It therefore stands in lieu of a report of operations, and it may be profitable to continue to quote from it to some extent. His alleged intention of withdrawing from Chancellorsville is thus explained. After setting forth that on the demolition of the Eleventh Corps, the previous evening, he threw Berry into the gap to arrest Jackson, "and if possible to seize, and at all hazards hold, the high ground abandoned by that corps," he says: —

"Gen. Berry, after going perhaps three-quarters of a mile, reported that the enemy was already in possession of the ground commanding my position, and that he had been compelled to establish his line in the valley on the Chancellorsville side of that high ground. As soon as this was communicated to me, I directed Gens. Warren and Comstock to trace out a new line which I pointed out to them on the map, and to do it that night, as I would not be able to hold the one I then occupied after the enemy should renew the attack the next morning."

" The position " at Dowdall's " was the most commanding one in the vicinity. In the possession of the enemy it would enable him with his artillery to enfilade the lines held by the Twelfth and Second Corps." " To wrest this position from the enemy after his batteries were established upon it, would have required slender columns of infantry, which he could destroy as fast as they were thrown upon it." Slender columns of infantry were at this time among Hooker's pet ideas.

" Every disposition was made of our forces to hold our line as long as practicable, for the purpose of being in readiness to co-operate with the movement which had been ordered to be made on our left."

" The attack was renewed by the enemy about seven o'clock in the morning, and was bravely resisted by the limited number of troops I could bring into action until eleven o'clock, when orders were given for the army to establish itself on the new line. This it did in good order. The position I abandoned was one that I had held at a disadvantage ; and I kept the troops on it as long as I did, only for the purpose of enabling me to hear of the approach of the force under Gen. Sedgwick." Thus much Hooker.

The position of both armies shortly after daybreak was substantially that to which the operation of Saturday had led.

The crest at Fairview was crowned by eight batteries of the Third and Twelfth Corps, snpported by Whipple's

Second brigade (Bowman's), in front to the left, forming, as it were, a third line of infantry.

In advance of the artillery some five hundred yards, (a good half-mile from the Chancellor House,) lay the Federal line of battle, on a crest less high than Fairview, but still commanding the tangled woods in its front to a limited distance, and with lower ground in its rear, deepening to a ravine on the south of the plank road. Berry's division held this line north of the plank road, occupying the ground it had fought over since dusk of the evening before. Supporting it somewhat later was Whipple's First brigade (Franklin's). Berdan's sharpshooters formed a movable skirmish-line; while another, and heavier, was thrown out by Berry from his own troops.

A section of Dimick's battery was trained down the road.

Williams's division of the Twelfth Corps was to the south of the plank road, both he and Berry substantially in one line, and perpendicular to it; while Mott's brigade was massed in rear of Williams's right.

Near Williams's left flank, but almost at right angles to it, came Geary's division, in the same intrenched line he had defended the day before; and on his left again, the Second Corps, which had not materially changed its position since Friday.

The angle thus formed by Geary and Williams, looked out towards cleared fields, and rising ground, surmounted by some farm-buildings on a high crest, about six hundred yards from Fairview.

At this farm, called Hazel Grove, during the night,

and until just before daybreak, holding a position which could have been utilized as an almost impregnable *point d'appui*, and which, so long as it was held, practically prevented, in the approaching battle, a junction of Lee's severed wings, had lain Birney's and Whipple's divisions. This point they had occupied, (as already described,) late the evening before, after Sickles and Pleasonton had finished their brush with Jackson's right brigades. But Hooker was blind to the fact that the possession of this height would enable either himself or his enemy to enfilade the other's lines; and before daybreak the entire force was ordered to move back to Chancellorsville. In order to do this, the intervening swamp had to be bridged, and the troops handled with extreme care. When all but Graham had been withdrawn, a smart attack was made upon his brigade by Archer of Hill's command, who charged up and captured the Hazel Grove height; but it was with no serious Federal loss, except a gun and caisson stalled in the swamp. Sickles drew in his line by the right, and was directed to place his two divisions so as to strengthen the new line at Fairview.

Reynolds's corps had arrived the evening before, and, after somewhat blind instructions, had been placed along the east of Hunting Run, from the Rapidan to the junction of Ely's and United-States Ford roads, in a location where the least advantage could be gained from his fresh and eager troops, and where, in fact, the corps was not called into action at all, restless however Reynolds may have been under his enforced inactivity.

The Eleventh Corps had gone to the extreme left, where

it had relieved Meade; Sykes was already formed on Reynolds's left, (having rapidly moved to the cross roads at dusk on Saturday;) while Meade with the rest of his corps, so soon as Howard had relieved him, went into position to support this entire line on the extreme right of the Army of the Potomac. Thus three strong army corps henceforth disappear from effective usefulness in the campaign.

The Confederate position opposite Fairview had been entirely rectified during the night to prepare for the expected contest. The division of A. P. Hill was now in the front line, perpendicular to the road. Archer on the extreme right, and McGowan, Lane, Pender, and Thomas, extending towards the left; the two latter on the north of the road. Heth was in reserve, behind Lane and Pender. Archer and McGowan were half refused from the general line at daylight, so as to face, and if possible drive Sickles from Hazel Grove. Archer was taking measures with a view to forcing a connection with Anderson; while the latter sent Perry by the Catharpen road, and Posey direct, towards the Furnace, with like purpose.

Colston was drawn up in second line with Trimble's division; while Rodes, who had led the van in the attack on Howard of last evening, now made the third. The artillery of the corps was disposed mainly on the right of the line, occupying, shortly after daylight, the Hazel-Grove crest, and at Melzi Chancellor's, in the clearing, where the Eleventh Corps had met its disaster.

There was thus opposed to the Federal right centre, (Berry's, Whipple's, and Birney's divisions of the Third Corps, and Williams's of the Twelfth,) consisting of about twenty-two thousand men, the whole of Jackson's corps, now reduced to about the same effective; while Anderson, on the left of the plank road, feeling out towards the Furnace, and McLaws on the right, with seventeen thousand men between them, confronted our left centre, consisting of Geary of the Twelfth, and Hancock of the Second Corps, numbering not much above twelve thousand for duty.

Owing to Hooker's ill-fitting dispositions, and lack of ability to concentrate, the fight of Sunday morning was thus narrowed to a contest in which the Federals were outnumbered, with the prestige of Confederate success to offset our intrenchments.

The right and left wings proper of the Union army comprised the bulk and freshest part of the forces, having opposite to them no enemy whatever, unless a couple of cavalry regiments scouting on the Mine and River roads.

Gen. Warren, who was much in Hooker's confidence, thus explains his understanding of the situation Saturday night: "The position of the Third Corps and our cavalry on the right flank of Jackson's cavalry" (? corps), "cut off, it seemed, all direct communication with Gen. Lee's right. No thought of retreating during the night was entertained on our side; and, unless the enemy did, the next day promised a decisive battle. By our leaving sufficient force in front of the right wing of the enemy to hold our breastworks, the whole of the rest of our force was to be thrown upon his left at dawn of day, with every prospect of annihilating it. To render this success more complete, Gen. Sedgwick, with the Sixth Corps, (about twenty thousand strong,) was to leave his position in front of the enemy's lines at Fredericksburg, and fall upon Gen. Lee's rear at daylight."

This summarizes an excellent plan, weak only in the fact that it was impracticable to expect Sedgwick to gain Lee's rear by daylight. The balance was well enough, and, vigorously carried out, could, even if unassisted by Sedgwick, scarcely fail of success.

To examine into its manner of execution.

XXII.

THE FIGHT AT FAIRVIEW.

A T the earliest dawn, while Rodes was issuing rations
to his men, who had been many hours without
food, the indefatigable Stuart gave orders for a slight
advance of his right, to reduce the angle of refusal or
Archer and McGowan; for at this moment it was ascertained that Sickles was being withdrawn from Hazel
Grove. By some error, Stuart's order was interpreted as
a command for the anticipated general attack, and the
advancing columns soon provoked the fire of the expectant Federals.

Seeing that the men were ready for their work, rations
or no rations, Stuart wisely refrained from recalling them;
and Berry and Williams betimes felt the shock of the
strong line of A. P. Hill, which Alexander seconded by
opening with his artillery in full action. The Confederates forged ahead with the watchword, "Charge, and
remember Jackson!" And this appeal was one to nerve
all hearts to the desperate task before them.

Hotchkiss thus describes the field of operations of this
morning: "The first line of works occupied by the
Federal troops had been thrown up in the night, and

was very formidable. The engineer division of the Union Army consisted of near four thousand men, and these had been unremittingly engaged in its construction. A vast number of trees had been felled, and formed into a heavy rampart, all approach to which was rendered extremely difficult by an abattis of limbs and brushwood. On the south side of the road this line is situated upon a ridge, on the Chancellorsville side of Lewis Creek, one of the numerous head-waters of the Mattapony. It is intersected by the smaller branches of this creek, and the ravines in which they run. These ravines extended behind the Federal lines, almost to the plank road, and afforded excellent positions for successive stands. In the morning, Sickles extended to the west of the creek, and held the elevated plateau at Hazel Grove. This is the most commanding point, except Fairview, in the vicinity. On the north of the plank road, the ground is more level. The line thus crossed several small branches, the origin of some small tributaries of the Rappahannock, but the ravines on that side are not considerable. From the ridge occupied by the first line, the ground falls away to the east, until the valley of another branch of Lewis Creek is reached. The depression here is considerable, and gives an abrupt slope to the Fairview hill, which rises directly from it on the eastern side. From the first line of the creek, extends on both sides of the road a dense forest. From the latter point to Fairview heights, and to Chancellorsville, on the south side of the road, the country is cleared. This clearing is bounded on the south by a drain, which runs from near Chancellorsville, between Fairview and the works occupied by Slocum. It extends some distance on the north of the road.

"Behind the front line of works, there were some defences in the valley near the creek, not constituting a connecting line, however; and these in turn were succeeded by the second main line of works, which covered the Fairview heights, and were more strongly constructed even than the first."

It was at just the time of Rodes's assault, that Birney had received orders to withdraw from his cardinal position at the angle made by Geary and Williams, and to form as a second and third line near the plank road, a duty there was an abundance of troops to fill. He retired, and ployed into brigade columns by regiments, immediately beyond the crest of Fairview hill. Here, placing batteries in position, he shelled the field from which he had just withdrawn. This crest, however, Archer speedily occupied; and on its summit Stuart, with better foresight than Hooker, posted some thirty guns under Walker, which enfiladed our lines with murderous effect during the remainder of the combat of Sunday, and contributed largely to our defeat.

The attack of the Confederates was made, "as Jackson usually did, in heavy columns" (*Sickles*), and was vigorous and effective. According to their own accounts, the onset was met with equal cheerful gallantry. While Archer occupied Hazel Grove, McGowan and Lane assaulted the works held by Williams, carried them with an impetuous rush, and pushed our troops well back. This rapid success was largely owing to a serious breach

made in the Union line by the decampment of the Third
Maryland Volunteers, a full regiment of Knipe's brigade,
which held the right of Williams's division on the plank
road. The regiment was composed of new men, no
match for Jackson's veterans. They stood as well as
raw troops can, in the face of such an onslaught; but
after a loss of about a hundred men, they yielded ground,
and were too green to rally. Into the gap thus made,
quickly poured a stream of Lane's men, thus taking
both Berry's and Williams's lines in reverse. The Second
Brigade was compelled to change front to meet this new
attack: Mott was instantly thrown forward to fill the
interval; and after a desperate hand-to-hand struggle he
regained the lost ground, and captured eight stands of
colors and about a thousand prisoners. This separated
Archer from the main line, and took in their turn Mc-
Gowan and Lane in reverse, precipitately driving them
back, and enabling our columns to regain the ground lost
by the fierceness of the Confederate inroad. This sally
in reverse likewise carried back Lane and Heth, the
entire corps having suffered severely from the excellent
service of the Federal guns. But the effect on Williams's
division of this alternating gain and loss, had been to
cause it to waver; while having for an instant captured
our works, was encouragement to our foes.

On the north of the road, Pender and Thomas had at
first won equal fortune against Berry's works, but their
success had been equally short-lived. For the falling-
back of Jackson's right, and the cheering of the Union
line as its fire advanced in hot pursuit, gave at the same

moment notice to the Confederate left that it was compromised, and to our own brave boys the news of their comrades' fortune. Pender and Thomas were slowly but surely forced back, under a withering fire, beyond the breastworks they had won. A second time did these veterans rally for the charge, and a second time did they penetrate a part of our defences; only, however, to be taken in flank again by Berry's right brigade, and tumbled back to their starting-point. But their onset had shown so great determination, that Ward was despatched to sustain Berry's right, lest he should be eventually over-matched.

The Federal line on the north of the plank road had thus doggedly resisted the most determined attacks of Jackson's men, and had lost no ground. And so hard pressed indeed was Pender by gallant Berry's legions, that Colquitt's brigade was sent to his relief. Pender's men had early expended all their ammunition, word whereof was sent to Stuart, but merely to evoke renewal of that stubborn officer's orders to hold their ground with the bayonet, and at all hazards. And such orders as these were wont to be obeyed by these hardened warriors.

The three Confederate lines of attack had soon, as on yesternight, become one, as each pushed forward to sustain the other. The enemy "pressed forward in crowds rather than in any regular formation" (*Sickles*); but the momentum of these splendid troops was well-nigh irresistible. Nichols's brigade of Trimble's division, and Iverson's and Rodes's of Rodes's division, pressed forward to sustain the first line on the north of the road, and repel the flank attack, constantly renewed by Berry. Another advance of the entire line was ordered. Rodes led his old brigade in person. The Confederates seemed determined, for Jackson's sake, to carry and hold the works which they had twice gained, and out of which they had been twice driven; for, with "Old Jack" at their head, they had never shown a sterner front.

Now came the most grievous loss of this morning's conflict. Gallant Berry, the life of his division, always in the hottest of the fire, reckless of safety, had fallen mortally wounded, before Ward's brigade could reach his line. Gen. Revere assumed command, and, almost before the renewal of the Confederate attack, "heedless of their murmurs," says Sickles's report, "shamefully led to the rear the whole of the Second Brigade, and portions of two others, thus subjecting these proud soldiers, for the first time, to the humiliation of being marched to the rear while their comrades were under fire. Gen. Revere was promptly recalled with his troops, and at once relieved of command." Revere certainly gives no satisfactory explanation of his conduct; but he appears to have marched over to the vicinity of French of the Second Corps, upon the White House clearing, and reported to him with a large portion of his troops. Revere was subsequently courtmartialled for this misbehavior, and was sentenced to dismissal; but the sentence was revoked by the President, and he was allowed to resign.

Col. Stevens was speedily put in command in Revere's stead; but he, too, soon fell, leaving the gallant division without a leader, nearly half of its number off the field, and the remainder decimated by the bloody contest of the past four hours.   Moreover, Gen. Hays, whose brigade of French's division had been detached in support of Berry, where it had done most gallant work, was at the same time wounded and captured by the enemy.

It was near eight o'clock.   The artillery was quite out of ammunition, except canister, which could not be used with safety over the heads of our troops.   Our outer lines of breastworks had been captured, and were held by the enemy.   So much as was left of Berry's division was in absolute need of re-forming.   Its supports were in equally bad plight.   The death of Berry, and the present location of our lines in the low ground back of the crest just lost, where the undergrowth was so tangled and the bottom so marshy, that Ward, when he marched to Berry's relief, had failed to find him, obliged the Federals to fall back to the Fairview heights, and form a new line at the western edge of the Chancellor clearing, where the artillery had been so ably sustaining the struggle now steadily in progress since daylight.   Sickles himself supervised the withdrawal of the line, and its being deployed on its new position.

The receding of the right of the line also necessitated the falling-back of Williams.   The latter officer had, moreover, been for some time quite short of ammunition; and though Graham had filled the place of a part of his line, and had held it for nearly two hours, repeatedly using the bayonet, Williams was obliged to give way before Stuart's last assault.   But Graham was not the man readily to accept defeat; and, as Williams's line melted away, he found himself isolated, and in great danger of being surrounded. Gen. Birney fortunately became aware of the danger before it was too late; and, hastily gathering a portion of Hayman's brigade, he gallantly led them to the charge in person; and, under cover of this opportune diversion, Graham contrived to withdraw in good order, holding McGowan severely in check.

The Union troops now establish their second line near Fairview. The Confederates' progress is arrested for the nonce. It is somewhat after eight A.M. A lull, premonitory only of a still fiercer tempest, supervenes.

But the lull is of short duration. Re-forming their ranks as well as may be on the south of the road, the Confederates again assault the Union second line, on the crest at Fairview. But the height is not readily carried. The slope is wooded, and affords good cover for an assault. But the artillery on the summit can now use its canister; and the Union troops have been rallied and re-formed in good order. The onset is met and driven back, amid the cheers of the victorious Federals.

Nor are Stuart's men easily discouraged. Failure only seems to invigorate these intrepid legions to fresh endeavors. Colston's and Jones's brigades, with Paxton's, Ramseur's, and Doles' of the third line, have re-enforced the first, and passed it, and now attack Williams with redoubled fury in his Fairview breastworks, while Birney sustains him with his last man and cartridge. The Confederate troops take all advantage possible of the numerous ravines in our front; but the batteries at Fairview pour a heavy and destructive fire of shell and case into their columns as they press on. Every inch of ground is contested by our divisions, which hold their footing at Fairview with unflinching tenacity.

Meanwhile Doles, moving under cover of a hill which protects him from the Federal batteries, and up a little branch coming from the rear of Fairview, takes in reverse the left of Williams's line, which has become somewhat separated from Geary, (whose position is thus fast becoming untenable,) moves up, and deploys upon the open ground at Chancellorsville. But he finds great difficulty in maintaining his footing, and would have at once been driven back, when Paxton's (old Stonewall) brigade comes up to his support on the double-quick. Jackson's spirit for a while seems to carry all before it; the charge of these two brigades against our batteries fairly bristles with audacity; but our guns are too well served, and the gallant lines are once again decimated and hustled back to the foot of the crest.

The seizure of Hazel Grove, from which Sickles had retired, had now begun to tell against us. It had enabled the Confederates not only to form the necessary junction of their hitherto separated wings, but to enfilade our lines in both directions. The artillery under Walker, Carter, Pegram, and Jones, was admirably served, and much better posted than our own guns at Fairview. For this height absolutely commanded the angle made by the lines of Geary and Williams, and every shot went crashing through heavy masses of troops. Our severest losses during this day from artillery-fire emanated from this source, not to speak of the grievous effect upon the *morale* of our men from the enfilading missiles.

About eight A.M., French, one of whose brigades, (Hays's,) had been detached in support of Berry, and who was in the rifle-pits on the Ely's Ford road near White House, facing east, perceiving how hotly the conflict was raging in his rear, on the right of the Third Corps line, and having no enemy in his own front, assumed the responsibility of placing four regiments of Carroll's brigade in line on the clearing, facing substantially west, and formed his Third Brigade on their right, supporting the left batteries of the Fifth Corps. This was a complete about-face.

Soon after taking up this position, Hooker ordered him forward into the woods, to hold Colquitt and Thomas in check, who were advancing beyond the right of Sickles's position at Fairview, and compromising the withdrawal to the new lines which was already determined upon. Says French: "In a moment the order was given. The men divested themselves of all but their fighting equipment, and the battalions marched in line across the plain with a steady pace, receiving at the verge of the woods the enemy's fire. It was returned with great effect, followed up by an impetuous charge. . . . The enemy, at first panic-stricken by the sudden attack on his flank, broke to the right in masses, leaving in our hands several hundred prisoners, and abandoning a regiment of one of our corps in the same situation."

But French had not driven back his antagonist to any considerable distance before himself was outflanked on his right by a diversion of Pender's. To meet this new phase of the combat, he despatched an aide to Couch for re-enforcements; and soon Tyler's brigade appeared, and went in on his right. This fight of French and Tyler effectually repelled the danger menacing the White House clearing. It was, however, a small affair compared to the heavy fighting in front of Fairview. And, the yielding of Chancellorsville to the enemy about eleven A.M. having rendered untenable the position of these brigades, they were gradually withdrawn somewhat before noon.

Still Jackson's lines, the three now one confused mass, but with unwavering purpose, returned again and again to the assault. Our regiments had become entirely depleted of ammunition; and, though Birney was ordered to throw in his last man to Williams's support, it was too late to prevent the latter from once more yielding ground.

For, having resisted the pressure of Stuart's right for nearly four hours, his troops having been for some time with empty cartridge-boxes, twenty-four hours without food, and having passed several nights without sleep, while intrenching, Williams now felt that he could no longer hold his ground. The enemy was still pressing on, and the mule-train of small ammunition could not be got up under the heavy fire. His artillery had also exhausted its supplies; Sickles was in similar plight; Jackson's men, better used to the bayonet, and possessing the momentum of success, still kept up their vigorous blows. Williams's line therefore slowly fell to the rear, still endeavoring to lean on Sickles's left.

Sickles, who had kept Hooker informed of the condition of affairs as they transpired, and had repeatedly requested support, now sent a more urgent communication to him, asking for additional troops. Major Tremaine reached headquarters just after the accident to Hooker, and received no satisfaction. Nor had a second appeal better results. What should and could easily have been done at an earlier moment by Hooker, — to wit, re-enforce the right centre (where the enemy was all too plainly using his full strength and making the key of the field), from the large force of disposable troops on the right and left, — it was now too late to order.

Before nine A.M., Sickles, having looked in vain for re-enforcements, deemed it necessary to withdraw his lines back of Fairview crest. Himself re-formed the divisions, except that portion withdrawn by Revere, and led them to the rear, where the front line occupied the late artillery breastworks. Ammunition was at once re-distributed.

We had doubtless inflicted heavy losses upon the Confederates. "Their formation for attack was entirely broken up, and from my headquarters they presented to the eye the appearance of a crowd, without definite formation; and if another corps had been available at the moment to have relieved me, or even to have supported me, my judgment was that not only would that attack of the enemy have been triumphantly repulsed, but that we could have advanced on them, and carried the day." (*Sickles.*)

On the Chancellorsville open occurred another sanguinary struggle. Stuart still pressed on with his elated troops, although his men were beginning to show signs of severe exhaustion. Franklin's and Mott's brigades, says Sickles, "made stern resistance to the impulsive assaults of the enemy, and brilliant charges in return worthy of the Old Guard."

But, though jaded and bleeding from this prolonged and stubbornly-contested battle, Jackson's columns had by no means relaxed their efforts. The blows they could give were feebler, but they were continued with the wonderful pertinacity their chief had taught them; and nothing but the Chancellor clearing, and with it the road to Fredericksburg, would satisfy their purpose.

And a half-hour later, Sickles, finding himself unsupported on right and left, though not heavily pressed by the enemy, retired to Chancellorsville, and re-formed on the right of Hancock, while portions of three batteries held their ground, half way between Chancellorsville and Fairview, and fired their last rounds, finally retiring after nearly all their horses and half their men had been shot, but still without the loss of a gun.

With characteristic gallantry, Sickles now proposed to regain the Fairview crest with his corps, attacking the enemy with the bayonet; and he thinks it could have been done. But, Hooker having been temporarily disabled, his successor or executive, Couch, did not think fit to license the attempt. And shortly after, Hooker recovered strength sufficient to order the withdrawal to the new lines at White House; and Chancellorsville was reluctantly given up to the enemy, who had won it so fairly and at such fearful sacrifice.

In retiring from the Chancellor clearing, Sickles states that he took, instead of losing, prisoners and material. This appears to be true, and shows how Stuart had fought his columns to the utmost of their strength, in driving us from our morning's position. He says: "At the conclusion of the battle of Sunday, Capt. Seeley's battery, which was the last battery that fired a shot in the battle of Chancellorsville, had forty-five horses killed, and in the neighborhood of forty men killed and wounded;" but "he withdrew so entirely at his leisure, that he carried off all the harness from his dead horses, loading his cannoneers with it." "As I said before, if another corps, or even ten thousand men, had been available at the close of the battle of Chancellorsville, on that part of the field where I was engaged, I believe the battle would have resulted in our favor." Such is the testimony of Hooker's warmest supporter. And there is abundant evidence on the Confederate side to confirm this assumption.

The losses of the Third Corps in the battle of Sunday seem to have been the bulk of that day's casualties.

There can be no limit to the praise earned by the mettlesome veterans of Jackson's corps, in the deadly fight at Fairview. They had continuously marched and fought, with little sleep and less rations, since Thursday morning. Their ammunition had been sparse, and they had been obliged to rely frequently upon the bayonet alone. They had fought under circumstances which rendered all attempts to preserve organization impossible. They had charged through tangled woods against well-constructed field-works, and in the teeth of destructive artillery-fire, and had captured the works again and again. Never had infantry better earned the right to rank with the best which ever bore arms, than this gallant twenty thousand,

— one man in every four of whom lay bleeding on the field.

Nor can the same meed of praise be withheld from our own brave legions. Our losses had been heavier than those of the enemy. Generals and regimental commanders had fallen in equal proportions. Our forces had, owing to the extraordinary combinations of the general in command, been outnumbered by the enemy wherever engaged. While we had received the early assaults behind breastworks, we had constantly been obliged to recapture them, as they were successively wrenched from our grasp, — and we had done it. Added to the prestige of success, and the flush of the charge, the massing of columns upon a line of only uniform strength had enabled the Confederates to repeatedly capture portions of our intrenchments, and, thus taking the left and right in reverse, to drive back our entire line. But our divisions had as often done the same. And well may the soldiers who were engaged in this bloody encounter of Sunday, May 3, 1863, call to mind with equal pride that each met a foeman worthy of his steel.

Say Hotchkiss and Allan: " The resistance of the Federal army had been stubborn. Numbers, weight of artillery, and strength of position, had been in its favor. Against it told heavily the loss of *morale* due to the disaster of the previous day."

XXIII.

THE LEFT CENTRE.

WHILE the bulk of the fighting had thus been done by the right centre, Anderson was steadily forcing his way towards Chancellorsville. He had Wright's, Posey's, and Perry's brigades on the left of the plank road, and Mahone's on the right, and was under orders to press on to the Chancellor clearing as soon as he could join his left to Jackson's right. He speaks in his report as if he had little fighting to do to reach his destination. Nor does Geary, who was in his front, mention any heavy work until about nine A.M.; for Geary's position was jeopardized by the enfilading fire of Stuart's batteries on the Hazel-Grove hill, and by the advance of Stuart's line of battle, which found his right flank in the air. He could scarcely be expected to make a stubborn contest under these conditions.

While thus hemmed in, Geary "obeyed an order to retire, and form my command at right angles with the former line of battle, the right resting at or near the Brick House," (Chancellorsville). While in the execution of this order, Hooker seems to have changed his purpose, and in person ordered him back to his original stand, "to hold it at all hazards."

In some manner, accounted for by the prevalent confusion, Greene's and Kane's brigades had, during this change of front, become separated from the command, and had retired to a line of defence north of the Chancellor House. But on regaining the old breastworks, Geary found two regiments of Greene's brigade still holding them.

Now ensued a thorough-going struggle for the possession of these breastworks, and they were tenaciously hung to by Geary with his small force, until Wright had advanced far beyond his flank, and had reached the Chancellor clearing; when, on instructions from Slocum, he withdrew from the unequal strife, and subsequently took up a position on the left of the Eleventh Corps.

Anderson now moved his division forward, and occupied the edge of the clearing, where the Union forces were still making a last stand about headquarters.

McLaws, meanwhile, in Couch's front, fought mainly his skirmishers and artillery. Hancock strengthened Miles's outpost line, who "held it nobly against repeated assaults."

While this is transacting, Couch orders Hancock to move up to the United-States Ford road, which he imagines to be threatened by the enemy; but the order is countermanded when scarcely begun. There is assuredly a sufficiency of troops there.

But Hancock is soon obliged to face about to ward off the advance of the enemy, now irregularly showing his line of battle upon the Chancellorsville clearing, while Sickles and Williams slowly and sullenly retire from before him.

The enemy is gradually forcing his way towards head-quarters. Hancock's artillery helps keep him in check for a limited period; but the batteries of Stuart, Anderson, and McLaws, all directing a converging fire on the Chancellor House, make it, under the discouraging circumstances, difficult for him to maintain any footing.

When Couch had temporarily assumed command, Hancock, before Geary was forced from his intrenchments by Anderson, disposed the Second Corps, with its eighteen pieces of artillery, in two lines, facing respectively east and west, about one mile apart. But Geary's relinquishment of the rifle-pits allowed the flanks of both the lines to be exposed, and prevented these dispositions from answering their purpose. Hancock clung to his ground, however, until the enemy had reached within a few hundred yards. Then the order for all troops to be withdrawn within the new lines was promulgated, and the removal of the wounded from the Chancellor House was speedily completed, — the shelling by the enemy having set it on fire some time before.

Hancock's artillery at the Chancellor House certainly suffered severely; for, during this brief engagement, Leppien's battery lost all its horses, officers, and cannoneers, and the guns had to be removed by an infantry detail, by hand.

The Confederate army now occupied itself in refitting its shattered ranks upon the plain. Its organization had been torn to shreds, during the stubborn conflict of the morning, in the tangled woods and marshy ravines of the Wilderness; but this had its full compensation in the possession of the prize for which it had contended. A new line of battle was formed on the plank road west of Chancellorsville, and on the turnpike east. Rodes leaned his right on the Chancellor House, and Pender swung round to conform to the Federal position. Anderson and McLaws lay east of Colston, who held the old pike, but were soon after replaced by Heth, with part of A. P. Hill's corps.

In the woods, where Berry had made his gallant stand opposite the fierce assaults of Jackson, and where lay by thousands the mingled dead and wounded foes, there broke out about noon a fire in the dry and inflammable underbrush. The Confederates detailed a large force, and labored bravely to extinguish the flames, equally exhibiting their humanity to suffering friend and foe ; but the fire was hard to control, and many wounded perished in the flames.

XXIV.

THE NEW LINES.

THE new lines, prepared by Gens. Warren and Comstock, in which the Army of the Potomac might seek refuge from its weaker but more active foe, lay as follows: —

Birney describes the position as a flattened cone. The apex touched Bullock's, (White House or Chandler's,) where the Mineral-Spring road, along which the left wing of the army had lain, crosses the road from Chancellorsville to Ely's Ford.

Bullock's lies on a commanding plateau, with open ground in its front, well covered by our artillery. This clearing is north of and larger than the Chancellor open, and communicates with it. The position of the troops on the left was not materially changed, but embraced the corps of Howard and Slocum. The right lay in advance of and along the road to Ely's, with Big Hunting Run in its front, and was still held by Reynolds. At the apex were Sickles and Couch.

The position was almost impregnable, and covered in full safety the line of retreat to United-States Ford, the road to which comes into the Ely's Ford road a half-mile west of Bullock's.

To these lines the Second, Third, and Twelfth Corps retired, unmolested by the enemy, and filed into the positions assigned to each division.

Only slight changes had been made in the situation of Meade since he took up his lines on the left of the army. He had, with wise forethought, sent Sykes at the double-quick, after the rout of the Eleventh Corps, to seize the cross-roads to Ely's and United-States Fords.   Here Sykes now occupied the woods along the road from Bullock's to connect with Reynolds's left.

Before daylight Sunday morning, Humphreys, relieved by a division of the Eleventh Corps, had moved to the right, and massed his division in rear of Griffin, who had preceded him on the line, and had later moved to Geary's left, on the Ely's Ford road.   At nine A.M., he had sent Tyler's brigade to support Gen. French, and with the other had held the edge of Chancellorsville clearing, while the Third and Twelfth Corps retired to the new lines.

And, when French returned to these lines, he fell in on Griffin's left.

About noon of Sunday, then, the patient and in no wise discouraged Union Army lay as described, while in its front stood the weary Army of Northern Virginia, with ranks thinned and leaders gone, but with the pride of success, hardly fought for and nobly earned, to reward it for all the dangers and hardships of the past few days.

Gen. Lee, having got his forces into a passable state of

re-organization, began to reconnoitre the Federal position, with a view to another assault upon it. It was his belief that one more hearty effort would drive Hooker across the river; and he was ready to make it, at whatever cost. But, while engaged in the preparation for such an attempt, he received news from Fredericksburg which caused him to look anxiously in that direction.

XXV.

SUNDAY'S MISCARRIAGE.

THE operations of Sunday morning, in common with many of our battles, furnish scarcely more than a narrative of isolated combats, having more or less remote or immediate effect upon each other.

The difficulty of the ground over which our armies were constantly called upon to manœuvre, explains " why the numerous bloody battles fought between the armies of the Union and of the secessionists should have been so indecisive. A proper understanding of the country, too, will help to relieve the Americans from the charge, so frequently made at home and abroad, of want of generalship in handling troops in battle, — battles that had to be fought out hand to hand in forests, where artillery and cavalry could play no part ; where the troops could not be seen by those controlling their movements ; where the echoes and reverberations of sound from tree to tree were enough to appall the strongest hearts engaged, and yet the noise would often be scarcely heard beyond the immediate scene of strife. Thus the generals on either side, shut out from sight and from hearing, had to trust to the unyielding bravery of their men till couriers from the different parts of the field, often extending for miles, brought word which way the conflict was resulting, before sending the needed support. We should not wonder that such battles often terminated from the mutual exhaustion of both contending forces, but rather, that, in all these struggles of Americans against Americans, no panic on either side gave victory to the other, like that which the French under Moreau gained over the Austrians in the Black Forest." (*Warren.*)

The Confederates had their general plan of action, viz., to drive their opponents from the Chancellor House, in order to re-unite their right and left wings, and to obtain possession of the direct road to Fredericksburg, where lay Early and Barksdale. To accomplish this end, they attacked the centre of Hooker's army, — the right centre particularly, — which blocked their way towards both objects.

It had been no difficult task to divine their purpose. Indeed, it is abundantly shown that Hooker understood it, in his testimony already quoted. But, if he needed evidence of the enemy's plans, he had acquired full knowledge, shortly after dawn, that the bulk of Stuart's corps was still confronting Sickles and Williams, where they had fought the evening before; and that Anderson and McLaws had not materially changed their position in front of Geary and Hancock. He could have ascertained, by an early morning reconnoissance, (indeed, his corps-commanders did so on their own responsibility,) that there was no enemy whatsoever confronting his right and left flanks, where three corps, the First, Fifth, and

Eleventh, lay chafing with eagerness to engage the foe. And the obvious thing to do was to leave a curtain of troops to hold these flanks, which were protected by almost insuperable natural obstacles, as well as formidable intrenchments, and hold the superfluous troops well in hand, as a central reserve, in the vicinity of headquarters, to be launched against the attacking columns of the enemy, wherever occasion demanded.

Hooker still had in line at Chancellorsville, counting out his losses of Saturday, over eighty-five thousand men. Lee had not exceeding half the number. But every musket borne by the Army of Northern Virginia was put to good use; every round of ammunition was made to tell its story. On the other hand, of the effective of the Army of the Potomac, barely a quarter was fought *au fond*, while at least one-half the force for duty was given no opportunity to burn a cartridge, to aid in checking the onset of the elated champions of the South.

Almost any course would have been preferable to Hooker's inertness. There was a variety of opportune diversions to make. Reynolds, with his fresh and eager corps, held the new right, protected in his front by Hunting Run. It would have been easy at any time to project a strong column from his front, and take Stuart's line of battle in reverse. Indeed, a short march of three miles by the Ely's Ford, Haden's Ford, and Greenwood Gold Mines roads, none of which were held by the enemy, would have enabled Reynolds to strike Stuart in rear of his left flank, or seize Dowdall's clearing by a *coup de main*, and absolutely negative all Stuart's efforts in front

of Fairview. Or an advance through the forest would
have accomplished the same end. To be sure, the ground
was difficult, and cut up by many brooks and ravines;
but such ground had been, in this campaign, no obstacle
to the Confederates. Nor would it have been to Reynolds, had he been given orders to execute such a manœuvre. Gen. Doubleday states in his testimony: "The
action raged with the greatest fury near us on our left."
"I thought that the simple advance of our corps would
take the enemy in flank, and would be very beneficial in
its results. Gen. Reynolds once or twice contemplated
making this advance on his own responsibility. Col.
Stone made a reconnoissance, showing it to be practicable."

The same thing applies to the Eleventh and portions of
the Fifth Corps on the left. A heavy column could have
been despatched by the Mine and River roads to attack
McLaws's right flank. Barely three miles would have sufficed, over good roads, to bring such a column into operating distance of McLaws. It may be said that the
Eleventh Corps was not fit for such work, after its defeat
of Saturday night. But testimony is abundant to show
that the corps was fully able to do good service early on
Sunday morning, and eager to wipe off the stain with
which its flight from Dowdall's had blotted its new and
cherished colors. But, if Hooker was apprehensive of
trusting these men so soon again, he could scarcely deem
them incapable of holding the intrenchments; and this
left Meade available for the work proposed.

Instead, then, of relying upon the material ready to his

hand, Hooker conceived that his salvation lay in the
efforts of his flying wing under Sedgwick, some fifteen
miles away. He fain would call on Hercules instead of
putting his own shoulder to the wheel. His calculations
were that Sedgwick, whom he supposed to be at Franklin's and Pollock's crossings, three or four miles below
Fredericksburg, could mobilize his corps, pass the river,
capture the heights, where in December a few Southern
brigades had held the entire Army of the Potomac at bay,
march a dozen miles, and fall upon Lee's rear, all in the
brief space of four or five hours. And it was this plan
he chose to put into execution, deeming others equal to
the performance of impossibilities, while himself could
not compass the easiest problems under his own eye.

To measure the work thus cut out for Sedgwick, by the
rule of the performances of the wing immediately commanded by Gen. Hooker, would be but fair. But Sedgwick's execution of his orders must stand on its own mer-
its. And his movements are fully detailed elsewhere.

An excuse often urged in palliation of Hooker's slug-
gishness, is that he was on Sunday morning severely disabled. Hooker was standing, between nine and ten A.M.,
on the porch of the Chancellor House, listening to the
heavy firing at the Fairview crest, when a shell struck
and dislodged one of the pillars beside him, which toppled
over, struck and stunned him; and he was doubtless for a
couple of hours incapacitated for work.

But the accident was of no great moment. Hooker
does not appear to have entirely turned over the command
to Couch, his superior corps-commander, but to have

merely used him as his mouthpiece, retaining the general direction of affairs himself.

And this furnishes no real apology. Hooker's thorough inability to grasp the situation, and handle the conditions arising from the responsibility of so large a command, dates from Thursday noon, or at latest Friday morning. And from this time his enervation was steadily on the increase. For the defeat of the Army of the Potomac in Sunday morning's conflict was already a settled fact, when Hooker failed at early dawn so to dispose his forces as to sustain Sickles and Williams if over-matched, or to broach some counter-manœuvre to draw the enemy's attention to his own safety.

It is an ungracious task to heap so much blame upon any one man. But the odium of this defeat has for years been borne by those who are guiltless of the outcome of the campaign of Chancellorsville; and the prime source of this fallacy has been Hooker's ever-ready self-exculpation by misinterpreted facts and unwarranted conclusions, while his subordinates have held their peace. And this is not alone for the purpose of vindicating the fair fame of the Army of the Potomac and its corps-commanders, but truth calls for no less. And it is desired to reiterate what has already been said, — that it is in all appreciation of Hooker's splendid qualities as a lieutenant, that his inactivity in this campaign is dwelt upon. No testimony need be given to sustain Hooker's courage: no man ever showed more. No better general ever commanded an army corps in our service: this is abundantly vouched for. But Hooker could not lead an hundred thousand men; and, unlike his predecessor, he was unable to confess it. Perhaps he did not own it to himself. Certainly his every explanation of this campaign involved the shifting of the onus of his defeat to the shoulders of his subordinates, — principally Howard and Sedgwick. And the fullest estimation of Hooker's brilliant conduct on other fields, is in no wise incompatible with the freest censure for the disasters of this unhappy week. For truth awards praise and blame with equal hand; and truth in this case does ample justice to the brave old army, ample justice to Hooker's noble aides.

The plan summarized by Warren probably reflected accurately the intentions of his chief, as conceived in his tent on Saturday night. It was self-evident that Anderson and McLaws could be readily held in check, so long as Jackson's corps was kept sundered from them. Indeed, they would have necessarily remained on the defensive so long as isolated. Instead, then, of leaving the Third Corps, and one division of the Twelfth, to confront Jackson's magnificent infantry, had Hooker withdrawn an entire additional corps, (he could have taken two,) and thrown these troops in heavy masses at dawn on Stuart, while Birney retained Hazel Grove, and employed his artillery upon the enemy's flank; even the dauntless men, whose victories had so often caused them to deem themselves invincible, must have been crushed by the blows inflicted.

But there is nothing at all, on this day, in the remotest degree resembling tactical combination. And, long before the resistance of our brave troops had ceased, all chances of successful parrying of Lee's skilful thrusts had passed away.

Hooker's testimony is to the effect that he was merely fighting on Sunday morning to retain possession of the road by which Sedgwick was to join him, and that his retiring to the lines at Bullock's was predetermined.

The following extract from the records of the Committee on the Conduct of the War, illustrates both this statement, and Hooker's method of exculpating himself by crimination of subordinates. "*Question to Gen. Hooker.* — Then I understand you to say, that, not hearing from Gen. Sedgwick by eleven o'clock, you withdrew your troops from the position they held at the time you ordered Gen. Sedgwick to join you.

"*Answer.* — Yes, sir; not wishing to hold it longer at the disadvantage I was under. I may add here, that there is a vast difference in corps-commanders, and that it is the commander that gives tone and character to his corps. Some of our corps-commanders, and also officers of other rank, appear to be unwilling to go into a fight."

But, apart from the innuendo, all this bears the stamp of an after-thought. If an army was ever driven from its position by fair fighting, our troops were driven from Chancellorsville. And it would seem, that, if there was any reasonable doubt on Saturday night that the Army of the Potomac could hold its own next day, it would have been wiser to have at once withdrawn to the new lines, while waiting for the arrival of Sedgwick. For here the position was almost unassailable, and the troops better massed; and, if Lee had made an unsuccessful assault, Hooker would have been in better condition to make a sortie upon the arrival of the Sixth Corps in his vicinity, than after the bloody and disheartening work at Fairview.

Still the inactivity of Hooker, when Sedgwick did eventually arrive within serviceable distance, is so entire a puzzle to the student of this campaign, that speculation upon what he did then actually assume as facts, or how he might have acted under any other given conditions, becomes almost fruitless.

XXVI.

SEDGWICK'S CHANGE OF ORDERS.

LET us return to the Sixth Corps of the Army of the Potomac, where operations now demanded Lee's undivided skill. This was properly the left wing of the army, which, under Sedgwick, had made the demonstration below Fredericksburg, to enable the right wing, under Hooker, to cross the river above, and establish itself at Chancellorsville. It had consisted of three corps; but, so soon as the demonstration had effected its purpose, it will be remembered that Hooker withdrew from Sedgwick's command both the First and Third Corps, leaving him with his own, the Sixth, to guard the crossings of the river; while Gibbon's division of the Second Corps did provost duty at the camp at Falmouth, and held itself in readiness to move in any direction at a moment's notice.

From this time on, the Sixth Corps may be more properly considered as a detached command, than as the left wing of the Army of the Potomac.

And, beyond some demonstrations in aid of Hooker's manœuvring, Sedgwick had been called on to perform no actual service up to the evening of May 2.

On May 1, a demonstration in support of Hooker's

advance from Chancellorsville had been ordered, and speedily countermanded, on account of the despatch having reached Sedgwick later than the hour set for his advance.

On the forenoon of May 2, Hooker had given Sedgwick discretionary instructions to attack the enemy in his front, "if an opportunity presents itself with a reasonable expectation of success."

Then came the despatch of 4.10 P.M., May 2, already quoted, and received by Sedgwick just before dark : —

" The general commanding directs that Gen. Sedgwick cross the river as soon as indications will permit; capture Fredericksburg with every thing in it, and vigorously pursue the enemy. We know the enemy is flying, trying to save his trains: two of Sickles's divisions are among them."

This despatch was immediately followed by another: " The major-general commanding directs you to pursue the enemy by the Bowling-Green road."

In pursuance of these and previous orders, Sedgwick transferred the balance of the Sixth Corps to the south side of the Rappahannock, one division being already there to guard the bridge-head. Sedgwick's orders of May 1 contemplated the removal of the pontoons before his advance on the Bowling-Green road, as he would be able to leave no sufficient force to guard them. But these orders were received so late as daylight on the 2d; and the withdrawal of the bridges could not well be accomplished in the full view of the enemy, without prematurely developing our plans.

The order to pursue by the Bowling-Green road having been again repeated, Sedgwick put his command under arms, advanced his lines, and forced the enemy — Early's right — from that road and back into the woods. This was late in the evening of Saturday.

On the same night, after the crushing of the Eleventh Corps, we have seen how Hooker came to the conclusion that he could utilize Sedgwick in his operations at Chancellorsville. He accordingly sent him the following order, first by telegraph through Gen. Butterfield, at the same time by an aide-de-camp, and later by Gen. Warren : —

HEADQUARTERS ARMY OF THE POTOMAC,
May 2, 1863, 9 P.M.

GEN. BUTTERFIELD.

The major-general commanding directs that Gen. Sedgwick crosses the Rappahannock at Fredericksburg on the receipt of this order, and at once take up his line of march on the Chancellorsville road until you connect with us, and he will attack and destroy any force he may fall in with on the road. He will leave all his trains behind, except the pack-train of small ammunition, and march to be in our vicinity at daylight. He will probably fall upon the rear of the forces commanded by Gen. Lee, and between us we will use him up. Send word to Gen. Gibbon to take possession of Fredericksburg. Be sure not to fail. Deliver this by your swiftest messenger. Send word that it is delivered to Gen. Sedgwick.

J. H. VAN ALEN,
Brigadier-General and Aide-de-Camp.

(Copy sent Gen. Sedgwick ten P.M.)

At eleven P.M., when this order of ten o'clock was

received, Sedgwick had his troops placed, and his dispositions taken, to carry out the orders to pursue, on the Bowling-Green road, an enemy indicated to him as in rapid retreat from Hooker's front; and was actually in bivouac along that road, while a strong picket-line was still engaged skirmishing with the force in his front. By this time the vanguard of his columns had proceeded a distance variously given as from one to three miles below the bridges in this direction; probably near the Bernard House, not much beyond Deep Creek.

It is to be presumed that the aide who bore the despatch, and reached Sedgwick later than the telegram, gave some verbal explanation of this sudden change of Hooker's purpose; but the order itself was of a nature to excite considerable surprise, if not to create a feeling of uncertainty.

Sedgwick changed his dispositions as speedily as possible, and sent out his orders to his subordinates within fifteen minutes after receipt of Hooker's despatch; but it was considerably after midnight before he could actually get his command faced about, and start the new head of column toward Fredericksburg.

Knowing the town to be occupied by the Confederates, Sedgwick was obliged to proceed with reasonable caution the five or six miles which separated his command from Fredericksburg. And the enemy appears to have been sufficiently on the alert to take immediate measures to check his progress as effectually as it could with the troops at hand.

Fredericksburg and the heights beyond were held by

Early's division and Barksdale's brigade, with an adequate supply of artillery, — in all some eighty-five hundred men. Sedgwick speaks, in his testimony before the
Committee on the Conduct of the War, as if he understood at this time that Early controlled a force as large as
his own; but he had been advised by Butterfield that the
force was judged to be much smaller than it actually was.

In his report, Early does not mention Sedgwick's advance on the Bowling-Green road, nor is it probable that
Sedgwick had done more than to advance a strong skirmish-line beyond his column in that direction. Early's
line lay, in fact, upon the heights back of the road, his
right at Hamilton's Crossing, and with no considerable
force on the road itself. So that Sedgwick's advance was
skirmishing with scouting-parties, sent out to impede his
march.

Early had received general instructions from Lee, *in case*
Sedgwick should remove from his front, to leave a small
force to hold the position, and proceed up the river to
join the forces at Chancellorsville. About eleven A.M. on
the 2d, this order was repeated, but by error in delivery
(says Lee) made *unconditional.* Early, therefore, left
Hays and one regiment of Barksdale at Fredericksburg,
and, sending part of Pendleton's artillery to the rear, at
once began to move his command along the plank road
to join his chief.

As this manœuvre was in progress, his attention was
called to the early movements of Sedgwick, and, sending
to Lee information on this point, he received in reply a
correction of the misdelivered order. He therefore about-
faced, and returned to his position at a rapid gait.

It is doubtful whether by daylight, and without any considerable opposition, Sedgwick could have marched the fifteen miles to Chancellorsville in the few hours allotted him. Nor is it claimed by Hooker that it was possible for Sedgwick to obey the order of ten P.M. literally; for it was issued under the supposition that Sedg-- wick was still on the north bank of the river. But Hooker does allege that Sedgwick took no pains to keep him informed of what he was doing; whence his incorrect assumption. To recross the river for the purpose of again crossing at Fredericksburg would have been a lame interpretation of the speedy execution of the order urged upon Sedgwick. He accordingly shifted his command, and, in a very short time after receiving the despatch, began to move by the flank on the Bowling-Green road towards Fredericksburg, Newton's division in the advance, Howe following, while Brooks still held the bridge-head.

It was a very foggy night; which circumstance, added to the fact that Sedgwick was, in common with all our generals, only imperfectly familiar with the lay of the land, and that the enemy, active and well-informed, enveloped him with a curtain of light troops, to harass his movement in whatever direction, materially contributed to the delay which ensued.

And Sedgwick appears to have encountered Early's pickets, and to have done some skirmishing with the head of his column, immediately after passing west of Franklin's Crossing, which, moreover, gave rise to some picket-firing all along the line, as far as Deep Run, where Bartlett confronted the enemy. As the outskirts of the town were entered, four regiments of Wheaton's and Shaler's brigades were sent forward against the rifle-pits of the enemy, and a gallant assault was made by them. But it was repulsed, with some loss, by the Confederates, who, as on Dec. 13, patiently lay behind the stone wall and rifle-pits, and reserved their fire until our column was within twenty yards. Then the regiments behind the stone wall, followed by the guns and infantry on the heights, opened a fire equally sudden and heavy, and drove our columns back upon the main body. The assault had been resolute, as the casualties testify, "one regiment alone losing sixty-four men in as many seconds" (*Wheaton*); but the darkness, and uncertainty of our officers with regard to the position, made its failure almost a foregone conclusion. This was about daylight. "The force displayed by the enemy was sufficient to show that the intrenchments could not be carried except at great cost." (*Sedgwick.*)

The officer by whom the order to Sedgwick had been sent, Capt. Raderitzchin, had not been regularly appointed in orders, but was merely a volunteer aide-de-camp on Gen. Hooker's staff.

Shortly after he had been despatched, Gen. Warren requested leave himself to carry a duplicate of the order to Sedgwick, (Capt. Raderitzchin being "a rather inexperienced, headlong young man,") for Warren feared the "bad effect such an impossible order would have on Gen. Sedgwick and his commanders, when delivered by him." And, knowing Warren to be more familiar with the country than any other available officer, Hooker detached him on this duty, with instructions again to impress upon Sedgwick the urgent nature of the orders. Warren, with an aide, left headquarters about midnight, and reached Sedgwick before dawn.

As daylight approached, Warren thought he could see that only two field-pieces were on Marye's heights, and that no infantry was holding the rifle-pits to our right of it. But the stone-wall breastworks were held in sufficient force, as was demonstrated by the repulse of the early assault of Shaler and Wheaton.

And Warren was somewhat in error. Barksdale, who occupied Fredericksburg, had been closely scanning these movements of Sedgwick's. He had some fourteen hundred men under his command. Six field-pieces were placed near the Marye house. Several full batteries were on Lee's hill, and near Howison's. And, so soon as Fredericksburg was occupied by our forces, Early sent Hays to re-enforce Barksdale; one regiment of his brigade remaining on Barksdale's right, and the balance proceeding to Stansbury's.

For, at daylight on Sunday, Early had received word from Barksdale, whose lines at Fredericksburg were nearly two miles in length, that the Union forces had thrown a bridge across the river opposite the Lacy house; and immediately despatched his most available brigade to sustain him.

Early's line, however, was thin. Our own was quite two and a half miles in length, with some twenty-two thousand men; and Early's eighty-five hundred overlapped both our flanks. But his position sufficiently counterbalanced this inequality. Moreover his artillery was well protected, while the Union batteries were quite without cover, and in Gibbon's attempted advance, his guns suffered considerable damage.

Brooks's division was still on the left of the Federal line, near the bridge-heads. Howe occupied the centre, opposite the forces on the heights, to our left of Hazel Run. Newton held the right as far as the Telegraph road in Fredericksburg.

Gibbon's division had been ordered by Butterfield to cross to Fredericksburg, and second Sedgwick's movement on the right. Gibbon states that he was delayed by the opposition of the enemy to his laying the bridge opposite the Lacy house, but this was not considerable. He appears to have used reasonable diligence, though he did not get his bridge thrown until daylight. Then he may have been somewhat tardy in getting his twenty-five hundred men across. And, by the time he got his bridge thrown, Sedgwick had possession of the town.

It was seven A.M. when Gibbon had crossed the river with his division, and filed into position on Sedgwick's right. Gibbon had meanwhile reported in person to Sedgwick, who ordered him to attempt to turn the enemy's left at Marye's, while Howe should open a similar movement on his right at Hazel Run. Gens. Warren and Gibbon at once rode forward to make a reconnoissance, but could discover no particular force of the enemy in our front. Just here are two canals skirting the slope of the hill, and parallel to the river, which supply power to the factories in the town. The generals passed the first canal, and found the bridge across it intact. The planks of the second canal-bridge had been removed, but the structure itself was still sound.

Gibbon at once ordered these planks to be replaced from the nearest houses. But, before this order could be carried out, Warren states that he saw the enemy marching his infantry into the breastworks on the hill, followed by a battery. This was Hays, coming to Barksdale's relief. But the breastworks contained a fair complement before.

Gibbon's attempt was rendered nugatory by the bridge over the second canal being commanded from the heights, the guns on which opened upon our columns with shrapnel, while the gunners were completely protected by their epaulements. And a further attempt by Gibbon to cross the canal by the bridge near Falmouth, was anticipated by the enemy extending his line to our right.

Gen. Warren states that Gen. Gibbon "made a very considerable demonstration, and acted very handsomely with the small force he had, — not more than two thousand men. But so much time was taken, that the enemy got more troops in front of him than he could master."

Gen. Howe had been simultaneously directed to move on the left of Hazel Run, and turn the enemy's right; but he found the works in his front beset, and the character of the stream between him and Newton precluded any movement of his division to the right.

By the time, then, that Sedgwick had full possession of the town, and Gibbon and Howe had returned from their abortive attempt to turn the enemy's flanks, the sun was some two hours high. As the works could not be captured by surprise, Sedgwick was reduced to the alternative of assaulting them in regular form.

It is not improbable that an earlier attack by Gibbon on Marye's heights, might have carried them with little loss, and with so much less expense of time that Sedgwick could have pushed beyond Salem Church, without being seriously impeded by troops sent against him by Gen. Lee.

And, as the allegation of all-but criminal delay on the part of Gen. Sedgwick is one of the cardinal points of Hooker's self-defence on the score of this campaign, we must examine this charge carefully.

Sedgwick asserts with truth, that all despatches to him assumed that he had but a handful of men in his front, and that the conclusions as to what he could accomplish, were founded upon utterly mistaken premises. Himself was well aware that the enemy extended beyond both his right and left, and the corps knew by experience the nature of the intrenchments on the heights.

Moreover, what had misled Butterfield into supposing, and informing Sedgwick, as he did, that the Fredericksburg heights had been abandoned, was a balloon observation of Early's march to join Lee under the mistaken orders above alluded to. The enemy was found to be alert wherever Sedgwick tapped him, and his familiarity with every inch of the ground enabled him to magnify his own forces, and make every man tell; while Sedgwick was groping his way through the darkness, knowing his enemy's ability to lure him into an ambuscade, and taking his precautions accordingly.

XXVII.

SEDGWICK'S ASSAULT.

NOW, when Sedgwick had concluded upon a general assault, he can scarcely be blamed for over-caution in his preparations for it. Four months before, a mere handful of the enemy had successfully held these defences against half the Army of the Potomac; and an attack without careful dispositions seemed to be mere waste of life. It would appear to be almost supererogatory to defend Sedgwick against reasonable time consumed in these precautions.

There had been a more or less continuous artillery-fire, during the entire morning, from our batteries stationed on either side of the river. This was now redoubled to prepare for the assault. Newton's batteries concentrated their fire on the stone wall, until our troops had neared it, when they directed it upon the crest beyond; while like action was effected to sustain Howe.

Instructions were issued to the latter, who at once proceeded to form three storming columns under Gen. Neill, Col. Grant, and Col. Seaver, and supported them by the fire of his division artillery.

Sedgwick at the same time ordered out from Newton's

division two other columns, one under Col. Spear, consisting of two regiments, supported by two more under Gen. Shaler, and one under Col. Johns of equal size, to move on the plank road, and to the right of it, flanked by a line under Col. Burnham, with four regiments, on the left of the plank road. This line advanced manfully at a double-quick against the rifle-pits, neither halting nor firing a shot, despite the heavy fire they encountered, until they had driven the enemy from their lower line of works, while the columns pressed boldly forward to the crest, and carried the works in their rear. All the guns and many prisoners were captured. This was a mettlesome assault, and as successful as it was brief and determined.

Howe's columns, in whose front the Confederate skirmishers occupied the railroad-cutting and embankment, while Hays and two regiments of Barksdale were on Lee's and adjacent hills, as soon as the firing on his right was heard, moved to the assault with the bayonet; Neill and Grant pressing straight for Cemetery hill, which, though warmly received, they carried without any check. They then faced to the right, and, with Seaver sustaining their left, carried the works on Marye's heights, capturing guns and prisoners wholesale.

A stand was subsequently attempted by the Confederates on several successive crests, but without avail.

The loss of the Sixth Corps in the assault on the Fredericksburg heights was not far from a thousand men, including Cols. Spear and Johns, commanding two of the storming columns.

The assault of Howe falls in no wise behind the one

made by Newton.   The speedy success of both stands out
in curious contrast to the deadly work of Dec. 13.   "So
rapid had been the final movement on Marye's hill, that
Hays and Wilcox, to whom application had been made
for succor, had not time to march troops from Taylor's
and Stansbury's to Barksdale's aid."   (*Hotchkiss and
Allan.*)

The Confederates were now cut in two : Wilcox and
Hays were left north of the plank road, but Hays retreated round the head of Sedgwick's column, and rejoined Early.   Wilcox, who, on hearing of Sedgwick's
manœuvres Sunday morning, had hurried with a portion
of his force to Barksdale's assistance at Taylor's, but had
arrived too late to participate in the action, on ascertaining Sedgwick's purpose, retired slowly down the plank
road, and skirmished with the latter's head of column.
And he made so determined a stand near Guest's, that
considerable time was consumed in brushing it away
before Sedgwick could hold on his course.

Early appears to deem the carrying of the Fredericksburg heights to require an excuse on his part.   He says
in his report about our preliminary assaults : "All his
efforts to attack the left of my line were thwarted, and
one attack on Marye's hill was repulsed.   The enemy,
however, sent a flag of truce to Col. Griffin, of the Eighteenth Mississippi Regiment, who occupied the works at
the foot of Marye's hill with his own and the Twenty-
first Mississippi Regiment, which was received by him
imperfectly ; and it had barely returned before heavy columns were advanced against the position, and the trenches

were carried, and the hill taken." "After this the artillery on Lee's hill, and the rest of Barksdale's infantry, with one of Hays's regiments, fell back on the Telegraph road; Hays with the remainder being compelled to fall back upon the plank road as he was on the left." Later, "a line was formed across the Telegraph road, at Cox's house, about two miles back of Lee's hill."

Barksdale says, "With several batteries under the command of Gen. Pendleton, and a single brigade of infantry, I had a front of not less than three miles to defend, extending from Taylor's hill on the left, to the foot of the hills in the rear of the Howison house."

Gen. Wilcox, he goes on to state, from Banks's Ford, had come up with three regiments as far as Taylor's, and Gen. Hays was also in that vicinity; but "the distance from town to the points assailed was so short, the attack so suddenly made, and the difficulty of removing troops from one part of the line to another was so great, that it was utterly impossible for either Gen. Wilcox or Gen. Hays to reach the scene of action in time to afford any assistance whatever. It will then be seen that Marye's hill was defended by but one small regiment, three companies, and four pieces of artillery."

Barksdale further states that, "upon the pretext of taking care of their wounded, the enemy asked a flag of truce, after the second assault at Marye's hill, which was granted by Col. Griffin; and thus the weakness of our force at that point was discovered."

The bulk of Early's division was holding the heights from Hazel Run to Hamilton's Crossing; and the sudden assault on the Confederate positions at Marye's, and the hills to the west, gave him no opportunity of sustaining his forces there. But it is not established that any unfair use was made of the flag of truce mentioned by Barksdale.

The loss in this assault seems heavy, when the small force of Confederates is considered. The artillery could not do much damage, inasmuch as the guns could not be sufficiently depressed, but the infantry fire was very telling; and, as already stated, both colonels commanding the assaulting columns on the right were among the casualties.

The enemy's line being thus cut in twain, sundering those at Banks's Ford and on the left of the Confederate line from Early at Hamilton's Crossing, it would now have been easy for Sedgwick to have dispersed Early's forces, and to have destroyed the depots at the latter place. But orders precluded anything but an immediate advance.

The question whether Sedgwick could have complied with his instructions, so as to reach Hooker in season to relieve him from a part of Lee's pressure on Sunday morning, is answered by determining whether it was feasible to carry the Fredericksburg heights before or at daylight. If this could have been done, it is not unreasonable to assume that he could have left a rear-guard, to occupy Early's attention and forestall attacks on his marching column, and have reached, with the bulk of his corps, the vicinity of Chancellorsville by the time the Federals were hardest pressed, say ten A.M., and most needed a diversion in their favor.

Not that Hooker's salvation in any measure depended on Sedgwick's so doing. Hooker had the power in his own hand, if he would only use it. But it should be determined whether Hooker had any legitimate ground for fault-finding.

Putting aside the question of time, Sedgwick's whole manœuvre is good enough. It was as well executed as any work done in this campaign, and would have given abundant satisfaction had not so much more been required of him. But, remembering that time was of the essence of his orders, it may be as well to quote the criticism of Warren : —

" It takes some men just as long to clear away a little force as it does a large one. It depends entirely upon the man, how long a certain force will stop him."

" The enemy had left about one division, perhaps ten thousand or twelve thousand men, at Fredericksburg, to watch him. They established a kind of picket-line around his division, so that he could not move any thing without their knowing it. Just as soon as Gen. Sedgwick began to move, a little random fire began, and that was kept up till daylight. At daylight, the head of Gen. Sedgwick's troops had got into Fredericksburg. I think some little attempt had been made to move forward a skirmish-line, but that had been repulsed. The enemy had considerable artillery in position."

" My opinion was, that, under the circumstances, the most vigorous effort possible ought to have been made, without regard to circumstances, because the order was peremptory." But this statement is qualified, when, in his examination before the Committee on the Conduct of the War, to a question as to whether, in his opinion, Gen. Sedgwick's vigorous and energetic attempt to comply with Hooker's order would have led to a different result of the battle, Warren answered: " Yes, sir! and I will go further, and say that I think there might have been more fighting done at the other end of the line. I do not believe that if Gen. Sedgwick had done all he could, and there had not been harder fighting on the other end of the the line, we would have succeeded."

If, at eleven P.M., when Sedgwick received the order, he had immediately marched, regardless of what was in his front, straight through the town, and up the heights beyond, paying no heed whatever to the darkness of the night, but pushing on his men as best he might, it is not improbable that he could have gained the farther side of this obstacle by daylight. But is it not also probable that his corps would have been in questionable condition for either a march or a fight? It would be extravagant to expect that the organization of the corps could be preserved in any kind of form, however slight the opposition. And, as daylight came on, the troops would have scarcely been in condition to offer brilliant resistance to the attack, which Early, fully apprised of all their movements, would have been in position to make upon their flank and rear.

Keeping in view all the facts, — that Sedgwick was on unknown ground, with an enemy in his front, familiar with every inch of it and with Sedgwick's every movement; that he had intrenchments to carry where a few months before one man had been more than a match for ten; that the night was dark and foggy; and that he was taken unawares by this order, — it seems that to expect him to carry the heights before daylight, savors of exorbitance.

But it may fairly be acknowledged, that more delay can be discovered in some of the operations of this night and morning, than the most rigorous construction of the orders would warrant. After the repulse of Wheaton and Shaler, a heavier column should at once have been thrown against the works. Nor ought it to have taken so long, under the stringency of the instructions, to ascertain that Gibbon would be stopped by the canal, and Howe by Hazel Run; or perhaps to organize the assaulting columns, after ascertaining that these flank attacks were fruitless.

All this, however, in no wise whatsoever shifts any part of the responsibility for the loss of this campaign, from Hooker's to Sedgwick's shoulders. The order of ten P.M. was ill-calculated and impracticable. Hooker had no business to count on Sedgwick's corps as an element in his problem of Sunday at Chancellorsville.

Sedgwick's movements towards his chief were certainly more rapid than those of Sickles on Saturday, and no one has undertaken to criticise the latter. Nor would Lee be lightly accused of tardiness for not attacking Sedgwick in force until Monday at six P.M., as will shortly be detailed, when he had despatched his advance towards him shortly after noon on Sunday, and had but a half-dozen miles to march. And yet Lee, precious as every moment was to him, consumed all these hours in preparing to assault Sedgwick's position in front of Banks's Ford.

In order to do justice to all sources of information, and show how unreliable our knowledge often was, it may be well to quote from Gen. Butterfield's testimony before the Committee on the Conduct of the War. "From the best information I had at the time the order came, there was not over a brigade of the enemy in the vicinity of Fredericksburg. This information was confirmed after wards by prisoners taken on Sunday by Gen. Sedgwick. They told me they were left there with orders, that, if they did not receive re-enforcements by a certain time, to withdraw; that they did withdraw about eleven o'clock on Saturday night, but met re-enforcements coming up, and turned back and re-occupied the works. The statement may have been false, or may have been true." It was clearly Early's march under his mistaken instructions, which the prisoners referred to. "If true, it would show that a bold movement of Gen. Sedgwick's command on Saturday night, would have taken Marye's heights, and put him well on the road towards Gen. Hooker before daylight." To the question whether the order could have been actually carried out: "There was a force of the enemy there, but in my judgment not sufficient to have prevented the movement, if made with a determined attack. Night attacks are dangerous, and should be made only with very disciplined troops. But it seemed to me at the time that the order could have been executed."

Gibbon, on the contrary, is of opinion that the strict

execution of the order was impracticable, but that probably an assault could have been made at daylight instead
of at eleven A.M. He recollects being very impatient
that morning about the delay, — not, however, being
more specific in his testimony.

XXVIII.

SEDGWICK MARCHES TOWARDS HOOKER.

SO soon as Sedgwick had reduced the only formidable works in his front, he made dispositions to push out on the plank road. Gibbon was left in Fredericksburg to prevent the enemy from crossing to the north side of the river, and to shield the bridges.

"Gen. Brooks's division was now given the advance, and he was farthest in the rear, not having got moved from the crossing-place." Brooks had so extensive a force in his front, that he was constrained to withdraw with extreme caution. "This necessarily consumed a considerable time, and before it was completed the sound of the cannonading at Chancellorsville had ceased." (*Warren.*)

This postponement of an immediate advance might well, under the stringency of the orders, have been avoided, by pushing on with the then leading division. Not that it would have been of any ultimate assistance to Hooker at Chancellorsville. At the time the storming columns assaulted Marye's heights, Hooker had already been driven into his lines at White House. And though none of his strictures upon Sedgwick's tardiness, as affecting his own situation, will bear the test of examination, time will not be considered wholly ill-spent in determining where Sedgwick might have been more expeditious. It no doubt accords with military precedents, to alternate in honoring the successive divisions of a corps with the post of danger; but it may often be highly improper to arrest an urgent progress in order to accommodate this principle. And it was certainly inexpedient in this case, despite the fact that Newton and Howe had fought their divisions, while Brooks had not yet been under fire.

" The country being open, Gen. Brooks's division was formed in a column of brigade-fronts, with an extended line of skirmishers in the front and flank in advance, and the artillery on the road." (*Warren.*) The New Jersey brigade marched on the right, and Bartlett's brigade on the left, of the road. This disposition was adopted that the enemy might be attacked as soon as met, without waiting for deployment, and to avoid the usual manœuvres necessary to open an action from close column, or from an extended order of march.

Gen. Newton followed, marching by the flank along the road. This "greatly extended the column, made it liable to an enfilading fire, and put it out of support, in a measure, of the division in advance." (*Warren.*)

Howe brought up the rear.

Meanwhile Wilcox, having arrested Sedgwick at Guest's, as long as his slender force enabled him to do, moved across country to the River road near Taylor's. But Sedgwick's cautious advance gave him the opportunity of sending back what cavalry he had, some fifty men, to skirmish along the plank road, while he himself moved his infantry and artillery by cross-roads to the toll-house, one-half mile east of Salem Church. Here he took up an admirable position, and made a handsome resistance to Sedgwick, until, ascertaining that McLaws had reached the crest at that place, he withdrew to the position assigned him in the line of battle now formed by that officer.

When Early perceived that Sedgwick was marching his corps up the plank road, instead, as he expected, of attacking him, and endeavoring to reach the depots at Hamilton's, he concentrated at Cox's all his forces, now including Hays, who had rejoined him by a circuit, and sent word to McLaws, whom he ascertained to be advancing to meet Sedgwick, that he would on the morrow attack Marye's heights with his right, and extend his left over to join the main line.

XXIX.

SALEM CHURCH.

IT was about noon before Lee became aware that Sedgwick had captured his stronghold at Fredericksburg, and was where he could sever his communications, or fall upon his rear at Chancellorsville. Both Lee and Early (the former taking his cue from his lieutenant) state that at first Sedgwick advanced down the Telegraph road, with an assumed purpose to destroy the line in Lee's rear, but that he was checked by Early. The nature, however, of Sedgwick's orders precluded his doing this, and there is no mention of such a purpose among any of the reports. And it was not long before Lee heard that Sedgwick was marching out towards the battle-ground in the Wilderness, with only Wilcox in his front.

McLaws, with his own three brigades, and one of Anderson's, was accordingly pushed forward at a rapid gait to sustain Wilcox; while Anderson, with the balance of his division, and fourteen rifled guns, was sent to the junction of the River road and Mine road to hold that important position. McLaws arrived about two P.M., and found Wilcox skirmishing, a trifle beyond Salem Church.

He was drawn back a few hundred yards, while Kershaw and Wofford were thrown out upon Wilcox's right, and Semmes and Mahone on his left. Wofford arrived somewhat late, as he had been temporarily left at the junction of the Mine and plank roads to guard them. McLaws's guns were concentrated on the road, but were soon withdrawn for lack of ammunition.

Some troops were thrown into Salem Church, and into a schoolhouse near by, in front of the woods, forming a salient; but the main Confederate line was withdrawn some three hundred yards within the wood, where a clearing lay at their back.

When Sedgwick's column reached the summit along the road, about a mile from Salem Church, Wilcox's cavalry skirmishers were met, and a section of artillery opened with solid shot from a point near the church, where Wilcox was hurrying his forces into line. The intervening ground was quite open on both sides the road. The heights at Salem Church are not considerable; but a ravine running north and south across its front, and as far as the Rappahannock, furnishes an excellent line of defence, and the woods come up to its edge at this point, and enclose the road.

Brooks was pushed in to attack the enemy, the main part of his division being on the left of the road, while Newton filed in upon his right, so soon as his regiments could be got up. Disposing his batteries (Rigby, Parsons, and Williston) along a crest at right angles to the road, not far from the toll-gate, where good shelter existed for the caissons and limbers, Brooks sharply advanced his lines under a telling fire, and, passing the undergrowth, penetrated the edge of the woods where lay Wilcox and Semmes and Mahone. Wilcox's skirmishers and part of his line gave way before Brooks's sturdy onset, which created no little confusion; but Wilcox and Semmes in person headed some reserve regiments, and led them to the charge. An obstinate combat ensues. Bartlett has captured the schoolhouse east of the church, advances, and again breaks for a moment the Confederate line. Wilcox throws in an Alabama regiment, which delivers a fire at close quarters, and makes a counter-charge, while the rest of his brigade rallies on its colors, and again presses forward. The church and the schoolhouse are fought for with desperation, but only after a heroic defence can the Confederates recapture them. Bartlett withdraws with a loss of two-fifths of his brigade, after the most stubborn contest. The line on the north of the road is likewise forced back. A series of wavering combats, over this entire ground, continues for the better part of an hour; but the enemy has the upper hand, and forces our line back towards the toll-house.

Though obstinately fighting for a foothold near the church, Brooks had thus been unable to maintain it, and he has fallen back with a loss of nearly fifteen hundred men. Reaching his guns, where Newton has meanwhile formed in support of his right, and where part of Howe's division later falls in upon his left, the enemy, which has vigorously followed up his retreat, is met with a storm of grape and canister at short range, the distance of our batteries from the woods being not much over five hundred yards. So admirably served are the guns, as Mc-Laws states, that it is impossible to make head against this new line; and the Confederates sullenly retire to their position near the church, which they had so successfully held against our gallant assaults, followed, but not seriously engaged, by a new line of Brooks's and Newton's regiments.

Wheaton's brigade manages to hold on in a somewhat advanced position on the right, where Mahone had been re-enforced from Wofford's line; but our left, after the second unsuccessful attempt to wrest more advanced ground from the enemy, definitely retires to a line a short mile from Salem Church.

The Confederate artillery had been out of ammunition, and unable to engage seriously in this conflict. Their fighting had been confined to the infantry regiments. But our own guns had borne a considerable share in the day's work, and had earned their laurels well.

It was now dark, and both lines bivouacked in line of battle.

Gen. Russell was placed in command of our front line.

The Union wounded were sent to Fredericksburg.

Gen. Warren, before the Committee on the Conduct of the War, passes the following comment upon this action: —

" Gen. Sedgwick carried the heights at Fredericksburg, and then moved on about three miles farther, and had a fight at Salem heights, but could not carry them. I think that by fighting the battle at Salem heights differently, we might have won that place also."

"Gen. Brooks carried Salem heights, but not being closely enough supported by other troops, he could not hold the heights. It was just one of those wavering things that a moment settles. If we had been stronger at that moment, we would have won; not being so, they won."

It is probable, that, had Brooks's attack been delayed until Newton and Howe could reach the scene, their support might have enabled him to keep possession of the ground he came so near to holding single-handed. But it was a dashing fight, deserving only praise; and it is doubtful whether the capture of Salem heights would have materially altered the event. It was the eccentric handling of the Chancellorsville wing which determined the result of this campaign. Sedgwick's corps could effect nothing by its own unaided efforts.

XXX.

SEDGWICK IN DIFFICULTY.

SO soon as Wilcox had retired from Banks's Ford to oppose Sedgwick's advance towards Chancellorsville, Gen. Benham threw a pontoon bridge, and established communications with the Sixth Corps. Warren, who up to this time had remained with Sedgwick, now returned to headquarters, reaching Hooker at eleven P.M., and, as a result of conference with him, telegraphed Sedgwick as follows : —

"I find every thing snug here. We contracted the line a little, and repulsed the last assault with ease. Gen. Hooker wishes them to attack him to-morrow, if they will. He does not desire you to attack again in force unless he attacks him at the same time. He says you are too far away for him to direct. Look well to the safety of your corps, and keep up communication with Gen. Benham at Banks's Ford and Fredericksburg. You can go to either place if you think best. To cross at Banks's Ford would bring you in supporting distance of the main body, and would be better than falling back to Fredericksburg."

And later : —

"I have reported your situation to Gen. Hooker. I find

192

that we contracted our lines here somewhat during the morning, and repulsed the enemy's last assault with ease. The troops are in good position. Gen. Hooker says you are separated from him so far that he cannot advise you how to act. You need not try to force the position you attacked at five P.M. Look to the safety of your corps. You can retire, if necessary, by way of Fredericksburg or Banks's Ford: the latter would enable you to join us more readily."

The former communication reached Sedgwick about four P.M. next day, and was the only one which up till then he had received. Warren, in his testimony before the Committee on the Conduct of the War, rather apologizes for the want of clear directions in this despatch, on the score of being greatly exhausted; but its tenor doubtless reflects the ideas of Gen. Hooker at the time, and is, indeed, in his evidence, fathered by Hooker as his own creation. It shows conclusively that there was then no idea of retiring across the river.

And it is peculiarly noteworthy, that, *at this time*, Hooker does not, in tone or by implication, reflect in the remotest degree upon Sedgwick, either for tardiness or anything else. Hooker was wont to speak his mind plainly. Indeed, his bluntness in criticism was one of his pet failings. And had he then felt that Sedgwick had been lacking in good-will, ability, or conduct, it is strange that there should not be some apparent expression of it. It was only when he was driven to extremity in explaining the causes of his defeat, that his after-wit suggested Sedgwick as an available scapegoat.

During the night, Lee came to the conclusion that he

must absolutely rid himself of Sedgwick, before he could again assault Hooker's defences. And, trusting to what he had already seen, in this campaign, of his opponent's lack of enterprise, he detailed Anderson's remaining three brigades to the forces opposing Sedgwick's wing, leaving only Jackson's corps, now numbering some nineteen thousand men, to keep Hooker, with his eighty thousand, penned up behind his breastworks, while himself repaired to the battle-ground of Monday at Salem Church, with the intention of driving Sedgwick across the river, so that he might again concentrate all his powers upon our forces near Chancellorsville.

By daylight Monday morning, Early advanced from his position at Cox's, and with very little difficulty recaptured the heights, held by only a few of Gibbon's men. Barksdale was again posted in the trenches, and instructed to keep Gibbon in check. Early meanwhile moved out to join McLaws, feeling our position with Smith's brigade, and ascertaining the left of our line to lie near Taylor's, and to extend from there down to the plank road.

At an early hour on Monday morning, it came to Sedgwick's knowledge, that the Confederates had re-occupied the heights in his rear, and cut him off from Fredericksburg, thus leaving him only Banks's Ford as a possible outlet in case of disaster. An attempt was made by Early to throw a force about Howe's left, and seize the approaches to the ford; but it was timely met, and repulsed by our men, who captured in this affair two hundred prisoners and a battle-flag. And, to forestall any serious movement to cut him off from Banks's Ford, Sedgwick had already formed Howe's division in line to the rear, extending, as we have seen, from the river to the plank road.

In his report, and particularly in his testimony before the Committee on the Conduct of the War, Howe speaks as if he had received from Sedgwick only general — in fact, vague — and rare instructions, as to the dispositions to be made of his division; and that all his particular manœuvres were originated and completed on his own responsibility, upon information, or mere hints, from headquarters of the corps. His line, over two miles long, was covered by less than six thousand men.

The despatch from Warren reached Sedgwick while matters were in this condition. To retire to Fredericksburg was impossible; to retire across Banks's Ford, except by night, equally so, unless he chose to hazard a disastrous attack from the superior force in his front. For Sedgwick had scarce twenty thousand men left to confront Lee's twenty-five thousand, and imagined the odds to be far greater. Our line was formed with the left on the river, midway between Fredericksburg and Banks's Ford, running southerly to beyond the plank road, following this on the south side for nearly two miles, and then turning north to the crest which Wheaton had held the night before. This was a long, weak position, depending upon no natural obstacles; but it was, under the circumstances, well defended by a skilful disposition of the artillery, under charge of Col. Tompkins. Gen. Newton's division held the right of this line, facing west; Gen.

Brooks had Russell's brigade, also posted so as to face west, on the left of Newton, while Bartlett and Torbert faced south, the former resting his left somewhere near Howe's right brigade. This portion of the line was, on Monday afternoon, re-enforced by Wheaton's brigade of Newton's division, withdrawn from the extreme right; and here it rendered effective service at the time the attack was made on Howe, and captured a number of prisoners. The bulk of Howe's division lay facing east, from near Guest's house to the river. The whole line of battle may be characterized, therefore, as a rough convex order, — or, to describe it more accurately, lay on three sides of a square, of which the Rappahannock formed the fourth. This line protected our pontoon-bridges at Scott's Dam, a mile below Banks's Ford.

No doubt Sedgwick determined wisely in preferring to accept battle where he lay, if it should be forced upon him, to retiring to Banks's Ford, and attempting a crossing in retreat by daylight.

Under these harassing conditions, Sedgwick determined to hold on till night, and then cross the river; having specially in view Hooker's caution to look well to the safety of his corps, coupled with the information that he could not expect to relieve him, and was too far away to direct him with intelligence.

Subsequent despatches instructed Sedgwick to hold on where he was, till Tuesday morning. These despatches are quoted at length on a later page.

Having re-occupied Fredericksburg heights, in front of which Hall's brigade of Gibbon's division was deployed as a skirmish-line, and occasionally exchanged a few shots with the enemy, Early communicated with McLaws, and proposed an immediate joint assault upon Sedgwick; but McLaws, not deeming himself strong enough to attack Sedgwick with the troops Early and he could muster, preferred to await the arrival of Anderson, whom he knew to be rapidly pushing to join the forces at Salem Church.

Anderson, who, prior to the receipt of his new orders, had been making preparations for a demonstration against Hooker's left at Chancellorsville, and had there amused himself by shelling a park of supply-wagons across the river, broke up from his position at the crossing of the Mine and River roads, headed east, and arrived about eleven A.M. at the battle-ground of Sunday afternoon. In an hour he was got into line on Early's left, while McLaws retained the crest he had so stubbornly defended against Brooks.

Lee now had in front of Sedgwick a force outnumbering the Sixth Corps by one-quarter, with open communications to Fredericksburg.

The general instructions issued by Lee, after a preliminary reconnoissance, were to push in Sedgwick's centre by a vigorous assault; and, while preparations were making for this evolution, a slight touch of the line was kept up, by the activity of the Confederate pickets in our front.

"Some delay occurred in getting the troops into position, owing to the broken and irregular nature of the ground, and the difficulty of ascertaining the disposition of the enemy's forces." (*Lee.*) But more or less steady skirmishing had been kept up all day, — to cover the disposition of the Confederate line, and if possible accurately to ascertain the position and relative strength of the ground held by Sedgwick's divisions.

Not until six P.M. were Lee's preparations completed to his satisfaction; but about that hour, at a given signal, the firing of three guns, a general advance was made by the Confederate forces. Early, on the right of the line, pushed in, with Hoke on the left of his division, from the hill on which Downman's house stands, and below it, Gordon on the right, up the hills near the intrenchments, and Hays in the centre.

On Early's left came Anderson, whose brigades extended — in order, Wright, Posey, Perry — to a point nearly as far as, but not joining, McLaws's right at about Shed's farm; Mahone of Anderson's division remained on McLaws's extreme left, where he had been placed on account of his familiarity with the country in that vicinity; and Wilcox occupied his ground of Sunday.

Alexander established his batteries on a prominent hill, to command the Union artillery, which was posted in a manner to enfilade McLaws's line. It was Alexander's opening fire which was the signal for the general assault.

The attack on the corner held by Brooks, was not very heavy, and was held in check chiefly by his skirmish-line and artillery. "The speedy approach of darkness prevented Gen. McLaws from perceiving the success of the attack until the enemy began to re-cross the river." "His right brigades, under Kershaw and Wofford, advanced through the woods in the direction of the firing, but the retreat was so rapid, that they could only join in the pursuit. A dense fog settled over the field, increasing the obscurity, and rendering great caution necessary to avoid collision between our own troops. Their movements were consequently slow." (*Lee.*)

Early's assault on Howe was made in *échelon* of battalions, and columns, and was hardy in the extreme. It was growing dark as the attack began, and Hays's and Hoke's brigades (says Early) were thrown into some confusion by coming in contact, after they crossed the plank road, below Guest's house. Barksdale remained at Marye's hill, with Smith on his left in reserve.

The weakness of Howe's long line, obliged that officer carefully to study his ground, and make arrangements for ready withdrawal to an interior line, if overmatched by the enemy; and he stationed his reserves accordingly. To the rear of the centre of his first line, held by Gen. Neill's brigade, and two regiments of Grant's, was a small covering of woods; here a portion of his reserves, and sufficient artillery, were concentrated. The main assault was made upon his left by Hoke and Hays. Their first onset was resolutely broken by Howe's firm front, though made with easy contempt of danger. The simultaneous attack upon his right was by no means so severe. It was speedily dashed back, and, by suddenly advancing this wing, Howe succeeded in capturing nearly all the Eighth Louisiana Regiment; but the gap produced by the over-advance of our eager troops, was shortly perceived by Gordon's brigade, which was enabled to move down a ravine in rear of Howe's right, and compelled its hasty withdrawal.

Meanwhile Neill's brigade, on Howe's left, was overpowered by Early's fierce and repeated onslaughts; but no wise disordered, though we had lost nearly a thousand men, it fell slowly and steadily back to the previously selected rallying-point, where, on being followed up by Hoke and Hays, the Vermont brigade, two regiments of Newton's division and Butler's regular battery, sent to Howe's support by Sedgwick, opened upon them so sharp a fire, that they retired in headlong confusion, largely increased by the approaching darkness. This terminated the fight on the left, and Howe's line was no further molested during the night.

Howe is clearly mistaken in alleging that his division was attacked by McLaws, Anderson, and Early. The position of these divisions has been laid down. It is one of those frequent assertions, made in the best of faith, but emanating solely from the recollection of the fierceness of a recent combat and from unreliable evidence.

XXXI.

SEDGWICK WITHDRAWS.

FORESEEING from the vigor of Lee's attack the necessity of contracting his lines, as soon as it was dark, Newton's and Brooks's divisions and the Light Brigade (Col. Burnham's), were ordered to fall rapidly back upon Banks's Ford, where they took position on the heights in the vicinity, and in Wilcox's rifle-pits. Howe was then quietly withdrawn, and disposed on Newton's right.

In his testimony before the Committee on the Conduct of the War, Gen. Howe appears to think that he was unfairly dealt with by Sedgwick; in fact, that his division was intentionally left behind to be sacrificed. But this opinion is scarcely justified by the condition of affairs and subsequent events.

Following are the important despatches which passed, during the latter part of these operations, between Hooker and Sedgwick: —

HEADQUARTERS SIXTH CORPS,
May 4, 1863, 9 A.M.

MAJOR-GEN. HOOKER.

I am occupying the same position as last night. I have secured my communication with Banks's Ford. The enemy are in possession of the heights of Fredericksburg in force. They appear strongly in our front, and are making efforts to drive us back. My strength yesterday morning was twenty-two thousand men. I do not know my losses, but they were large, probably five thousand men. I cannot use the cavalry. It depends upon the condition and position of your force whether I can sustain myself here. Howe reports the enemy advancing upon Fredericksburg.

JOHN SEDGWICK, Major-General.

SEDGWICK'S HEADQUARTERS, NEAR BANKS'S FORD, VA.,
May 4, 1863, 9.45 A.M.

GEN. HOOKER.

The enemy are pressing me. I am taking position to cross the river wherever (? whenever) necessary.

J. SEDGWICK, Major-General.

HEADQUARTERS ARMY OF THE POTOMAC,
May 4, 1863, 10.30 A.M.

GEN. SEDGWICK,

    Commanding Sixth Corps.

The commanding general directs that in the event you fall back, you reserve, if practicable, a position on the Fredericksburg side of the Rappahannock, which you can hold securely until to-morrow P.M. Please let the commanding general have your opinion in regard to this by telegraph from Banks's Ford as soon as possible.

S. WILLIAMS,
Assistant Adjutant-General.

HEADQUARTERS ARMY OF THE POTOMAC,
CHANCELLORSVILLE, VA., May 4, 1863, 11 A.M.

MAJOR-GEN. SEDGWICK.

The major-general commanding directs me to say that he does not wish you to cross the river at Banks's Ford unless you are compelled to do so. The batteries at Banks's Ford command the position. If it is practicable for you to maintain a position south side of Rappahannock, near Banks's Ford, you will do so. It is very important that we retain position at Banks's Ford. Gen. Tyler commands the reserve artillery there.

J. H. VAN ALEN,

Brigadier-General and Aide-de-Camp.

SIXTH CORPS, May 4, 1863, 11 A.M.

MAJOR-GEN. BUTTERFIELD AND GEN. HOOKER.

I hold the same position. The enemy are pressing me hard. If I can hold until night, I shall cross at Banks's Ford, under instructions from Gen. Hooker, given by Brig.-Gen. Warren.

JOHN SEDGWICK, *Major-General.*

SEDGWICK'S HEADQUARTERS, May 4, 1863, 11.15 A.M.

MAJOR-GEN. HOOKER.

The enemy threatens me strongly on two fronts. My position is bad for such attack. It was assumed for attack, and not for defence. It is not improbable that bridges at Banks's Ford may be sacrificed. Can you help me strongly if I am attacked?

JOHN SEDGWICK, *Major-General.*

P. S. — My bridges are two miles from me. I am compelled to cover them above and below from attack, with the additional assistance of Gen. Benham's brigade alone. J. S.

HEADQUARTERS ARMY OF THE POTOMAC,

CHANCELLORSVILLE, VA., May 4, 1863, 11.50 A.M.

MAJOR-GEN. SEDGWICK.

If the necessary information shall be obtained to-day, and if it shall be of the character he anticipates, it is the intention of the general to advance to-morrow. In this event the position of your corps on the south side of the Rappahannock will be as favorable as the general could desire. It is for this reason he desires that your troops may not cross the Rappahannock.

J. H. VAN ALEN,
Brigadier-General and Aide-de-Camp.

HEADQUARTERS ARMY OF THE POTOMAC,
May 4, 1863, 1.20 P.M.

GEN. SEDGWICK,
    Commanding Sixth Corps.

I expect to advance to-morrow morning, which will be likely to relieve you. You must not count on much assistance without I hear heavy firing. Tell Gen. Benham to put down the other bridge if you desire it.

J. HOOKER, *Major-General.*

HEADQUARTERS SIXTH CORPS,
May 4, 1863, 1.40 P.M.

MAJOR-GEN. HOOKER.

I occupy the same position as yesterday when Gen. Warren left me. I have no means of judging enemy's force about me — deserters say forty thousand. I shall take a position near Banks's Ford, and near the Taylor house, at the suggestion of Gen. Warren ; officers have already gone to select a position. It is believed that the heights of Fredericksburg are occupied by two divisions of the enemy.

JOHN SEDGWICK, *Major-General.*

May 4, 1863. (Hour not stated.)

MAJOR-GEN. SEDGWICK,
    Banks's Ford, Va.

It is of vital importance that you should take a commanding position near Fredericksburg, which you can hold to a certainty till to-morrow. Please advise me what you can do in this respect. I enclose substance of a communication sent last night. Its suggestions are highly important, and meet my full approval. There are positions on your side commanded by our batteries on the other side I think you could take and hold. The general would recommend as one such position the ground on which Dr. Taylor's is situated.

GEN. HOOKER. (?)

May 4, 1863, 2.15 P.M.

GEN. HOOKER.

I shall do my utmost to hold a position on the right bank of the Rappahannock until to-morrow.

JOHN SEDGWICK, *Major-General.*

BANKS'S FORD, VA.,
May 4, 1863, 11.50 P.M. (Received 1 A.M., May 5.)

GEN. HOOKER,
    United-States Ford.

My army is hemmed in upon the slope, covered by the guns from the north side of Banks's Ford. If I had only this army to care for, I would withdraw it to-night. Do your operations require that I should jeopard it by retaining it here? An immediate reply is indispensable, or I may feel obliged to withdraw.

JOHN SEDGWICK, *Major-General.*

BANKS'S FORD, VA.,
May 5, 1863. (Received 1 A.M.)

GEN. HOOKER.

I shall hold my position as ordered on south of Rappahannock.

SEDGWICK.

HEADQUARTERS,

May 5, 1863, 1 A.M.   (Received 2 A.M.)

GEN. SEDGWICK.

Despatch this moment received. Withdraw. Cover the river, and prevent any force crossing. Acknowledge this.

By command of Major-Gen. Hooker.

DANL. BUTTERFIELD

HEADQUARTERS,

May 5, 1863, 1.20 A.M.

GEN. SEDGWICK.

Yours received saying you should hold position. Order to withdraw countermanded. Acknowledge both.

GEN. HOOKER.

BANKS'S FORD, VA.,

May 5, 1863, 2 P.M. (should be 2 A.M.).

MAJOR-GEN. BUTTERFIELD.

Gen. Hooker's order received. Will withdraw my forces immediately.

JOHN SEDGWICK, *Major-General.*

HEADQUARTERS SIXTH CORPS,

May 5, 1863, 7 A.M.

GEN. BUTTERFIELD.

I recrossed to the north bank of the Rappahannock last night, and am in camp about a mile back from the ford. The bridges have been taken up.

JOHN SEDGWICK, *Major-General.*

These despatches explain themselves, if read, as is indispensable, with the hours of sending and receipt kept well in mind. No fault can be imputed to either Hooker or Sedgwick, in that the intention of the one could not be executed by the other. The apparent cross-purpose of the despatches is explained by the difficulty of communication between headquarters and the Sixth Corps.

The order to withdraw, though sent by Hooker before the receipt of Sedgwick's despatch saying he would hold the corps south of the river, was received by Sedgwick long before the countermand, which was exceptionally delayed, and was at once, under the urgent circumstances, put into course of execution.

As soon as the enemy ascertained that Sedgwick was crossing, Alexander's artillery began dropping shells in the neighborhood of the bridges and river banks; and Gen. Wilcox, with his own and Kershaw's brigades, followed up Sedgwick's movements to the crossing, and used his artillery freely.

When the last column had almost filed upon the bridge, Sedgwick was taken aback by the receipt of Hooker's despatch of 1.20 A.M., countermanding the order to withdraw as above quoted.

The main portion, however, being already upon the left bank, the corps could not now re-cross, except by forcing the passage, as the Confederates absolutely commanded the bridge and approaches, and with a heavy body of troops. And, as Lee was fully satisfied to have got rid of Sedgwick, upon conditions which left him free to turn with the bulk of his army upon Hooker, it was not likely that Sedgwick could in any event have successfully attempted it. The situation left him no choice but to go into camp near by. An adequate force was sent to watch the ford, and guard the river.

The losses of the Sixth Corps during these two days' engagements were 4,925 men. Sedgwick captured, according to his report, five flags, fifteen guns (nine of which were brought off), and fourteen hundred prisoners, and lost no material. These captures are not conceded by the Confederate authorities, some of whom claim that Sedgwick decamped in such confusion as to leave the ground strewed with arms, accoutrements, and material of all kinds. But it is probable, on comparison of all facts, and the due weighing of all testimony, that substantially nothing was lost by the Sixth Corps, except a part of the weapons of the dead and wounded.

Gibbon's division, about the same time, crossed to the north bank of the river, and the pontoon bridge at Lacy's was taken up. Warren says, " Gen. Sedgwick was attacked very heavily on Monday, fought all day, and retreated across the river that night. We lay quiet at Chancellorsville pretty nearly all day." This Warren plainly esteems a poor sample of generalship, and he does not understand why Hooker did not order an assault. " I think it very probable we could have succeeded if it had been made." " Gen. Hooker appeared very much exhausted," — " 'tired' would express it."

Lee's one object having been to drive Sedgwick across the river, so as to be relieved of the troublesome insecurity of his rear, he could now again turn his undivided attention to his chief enemy, who lay listlessly expectant at Chancellorsville, and apparently oblivious of his maxim enjoined upon Stoneman, " that celerity, audacity, and resolution are every thing in war."

Early and Barksdale were left, as before, to hold the Confederate lines at and near Fredericksburg, while Mc-Laws and Anderson were at once ordered back to the old battle-field. "They reached their destination during the afternoon (Tuesday, 5th) in the midst of a violent storm, which continued throughout the night, and most of the following day." (*Lee.*)

Wilcox and Wright lay that night in bivouac on the Catherine road; Mahone, Posey, and Perry, along the plank road.

Kershaw was sent to relieve Heth at the crossing of the River and Mine roads, and the latter rejoined his division.

The night of Tuesday Lee spent in preparations to assault Hooker's position at daylight on Wednesday. The Confederate scouts had been by no means idle; and the position occupied by Hooker, in most of its details, was familiar to the Southern commander. He was thus able to develop his plans with greater ease than a less familiarity with the *terrain* would have yielded. He was satisfied that one more vigorous blow would disable his antagonist for this campaign, and he was unwilling to delay in striking it.

XXXII.

HOOKER'S CRITICISMS.

L ET us now examine into Hooker's various criticisms upon Sedgwick's conduct.

Hooker, in his testimony before the Committee on the Conduct of the War, baldly accuses Sedgwick of neglecting to keep him advised of his movements, the inference being that he was debarred thereby from intelligently using him; and states that when he sent Sedgwick the despatch to join him at Chancellorsville, "it was written under the impression that his corps was on the north side of the Rappahannock." But could Hooker rationally assume this to be the case when he had, five hours before, ordered Sedgwick to cross and pursue a flying enemy, and well knew that he had a portion of his forces already guarding the bridge-heads on the Fredericksburg side ?

"The night was so bright that . . . no special difficulty was apprehended in executing the order." In the vicinity of Fredericksburg, shortly after midnight, a fog appears to have arisen from the river, which considerably impeded the movements of the Sixth Corps. This Hooker knew from Sedgwick's report, which he was bound to believe, unless evidence existed to show the contrary. "As will

be seen, the order was peremptory, and would have justified him in losing every man of his command in its
execution."

Hooker also states that Warren was sent to Sedgwick
on account of his familiarity with the ground, and to
impress upon the latter the necessity of strict compliance
with the order.

"I supposed, and am still of the opinion, that, if Gen.
Sedgwick's men had shouldered arms and advanced at
the time named, he would have encountered less resistance and suffered less loss; but, as it was, it was late when
he went into Fredericksburg, and before he was in readiness to attack the heights in rear of the town, which was
about eleven o'clock A.M. on the 3d, the enemy had observed his movement, and concentrated almost their entire
force at that point to oppose him." "He had the whole
force of the enemy there to run against in carrying the
heights beyond Fredericksburg, but he carried them with
ease; and, by his movements after that, I think no one
would infer that he was confident in himself, and the
enemy took advantage of it. I knew Gen. Sedgwick very
well: he was a classmate of mine, and I had been through
a great deal of service with him. He was a perfectly
brave man, and a good one; but when it came to manœuvring troops, or judging of positions for them, in my
judgment he was not able or expert. Had Gen. Reynolds been left with that independent command, I have
no doubt the result would have been very different."
"When the attack was made, it had to be upon the
greater part of the enemy's force left on the right: never-

theless the troops advanced, carried the heights without heavy loss, and leisurely took up their line of march on the plank road, advancing two or three miles that day."

Now, this is scarcely a fair statement of facts. And yet they were all spread before Hooker, in the reports of the Sixth Corps and of Gibbon. No doubt Sedgwick was bound, as far as was humanly possible, to obey that order; but, as in "losing every man in his command" in its execution, he would scarcely have been of great eventual utility to his chief, he did the only wise thing, in exercising ordinary discretion as to the method of attacking the enemy in his path. Hooker's assumption that Sedgwick was on the north side of the Rappahannock was his own, and not Sedgwick's fault. Hooker might certainly have supposed that Sedgwick had obeyed his previous orders, in part at least.

Sedgwick testified before the Committee on the Conduct of the War: "I have understood that evidence has appeared before the Committee censuring me very much for not being at Chancellorsville at daylight, in accordance with the order of Gen. Hooker. I now affirm that it was impossible to have made the movement, if there had not been a rebel soldier in front of me."

"I lost a thousand men in less than ten minutes time in taking the heights of Fredericksburg."

Sedgwick did "shoulder arms and advance" as soon as he received the order; but the reports show plainly enough that he encountered annoying opposition so soon as he struck the outskirts of the town; that he threw forward assaulting columns at once; and that these fought as well as the conditions warranted, but were repulsed.

It is not intended to convey the impression that there was no loss of time on Sedgwick's part. On the contrary, he might certainly have been more active in some of his movements. No doubt there were other general officers who would have been. But it is no exaggeration to insist that his dispositions were fully as speedy as those of any other portion of the army in this campaign.

Hooker not only alleges that " in his judgment, Gen. Sedgwick did not obey the spirit of his order, and made no sufficient effort to obey it," but quotes Warren as saying that Sedgwick " would not have moved at all if he [Warren] had not been there; and that, when he did move, it was not with sufficient confidence or ability on his part to manœuvre his troops." It is very doubtful whether Warren ever put his opinion in so strong a way as thus quoted by Hooker from memory. His report does speak of Gibbon's slowness in coming up, and of his thus losing the chance of crossing the canals and taking the breastworks before the Confederates filed into them. But beyond a word to the effect that giving the advance to Brooks's division, after the capture of the heights, "necessarily consumed a considerable time," Warren does not in his report particularly criticise Sedgwick's movements. And in another place he does speak of the order of ten P.M. as an " impossible " one.

Gen. Warren's testimony on this subject is of the highest importance, as representing Gen. Hooker in person. As before stated, he carried a duplicate of Hooker's order of ten P.M., to Sedgwick, with instructions from the general to urge upon Sedgwick the importance of the utmost celerity. Moreover, Warren knew the country better than any one else, and was more generally conversant with Hooker's plans, ideas, and methods, being constantly at his side. "Gen. Sedgwick was ordered to be in his position by daylight: of course that implied, if he could be there."

"If Sedgwick had got to Chancellorsville by daylight, I think we ought to have destroyed Lee's army. But it would depend a great deal upon how hard the other part of the army fought; for Gen. Sedgwick, with his twenty thousand men, was in great danger of being destroyed if he became isolated."

Moreover, Hooker in this testimony says: "Early in the campaign I had come to the conclusion that with the arms now in use it would be impossible to carry works by an assault in front, provided they were properly constructed and properly manned;" and refers to the Fredericksburg assault of Dec. 13, to illustrate this position, saying that they (the enemy) "could destroy men faster than I could throw them on the works;" and, "I do not know of an instance when rifle-pits, properly constructed and properly manned, have been taken by front assaults alone."

And yet his order to Sedgwick was (as he construes it), blindly to throw himself into this impossible situation, and lose every man in his command rather than not make the attempt at once, and without waiting properly to dispose his men, or feel the enemy.

As to the leisurely marching of two or three miles on

Sunday, we have seen how Brooks's march was summarily arrested at Salem Church, and how his attempt to force a passage, cost him alone some fifteen hundred men.

There is a good deal of evidence difficult to deal with in this movement of the Sixth Corps. The report of Gen. Howe, written immediately after the campaign, states facts dispassionately, and is to the point and nothing more. This is as it should be in the report of a general to his superior. It has but one error of consequence, viz., the assumption that the three divisions of Anderson, McLaws, and Early, all under command of Gen. Lee, attacked his line, leaving no force in front of Brooks and Newton. It was Early alone, or Early assisted by a brigade of Anderson, who attacked Howe.

But his testimony a year later, before the Committee on the Conduct of the War, cannot be commended as dispassionate, and contains serious errors. Gen. Howe states that the order to advance towards Chancellorsville was received "just after dark, say eight o'clock," whereas it was not sent until nine P.M. from Chancellorsville, and ten P.M. from Falmouth; nor did Sedgwick receive it until eleven P.M. Howe evidently remembered the order to pursue by the Bowling-Green road, as the one to march to Chancellorsville, — when speaking of time of delivery. The deductions Gen. Howe makes from errors like this are necessarily somewhat warped. But let us give all due weight to the testimony of an able soldier. He states that his attack on Marye's heights was made on a mere notice from Sedgwick, that he was about to attack, and desired Howe to assist; that he received on Sunday evening a bare intimation only from Sedgwick, that the left of the corps must be protected, and that he consequently moved his own left round to the river; and later, that Sedgwick sent him word to strengthen his position for defence; but complains that Sedgwick did not properly look after his division. "Not receiving any instruction or assistance from Gen. Sedgwick, I felt that we were left to take care of ourselves. It seemed to me, from the movements or arrangements made during the day, that there was a want of appreciation or a misunderstanding of the position which we held." Sedgwick's entire confidence in Howe's ability to handle his division, upon general instructions of the object to be attained, might account fully for a large part of this apparent vagueness. But Howe does not look at it in this light. His opinion was, that no necessity existed for the Sixth Corps to fall back across the river.

Gen. Howe's testimony is very positive as to the possibility of the Sixth Corps complying with Hooker's order as given. He thinks a night attack could have been made on the Fredericksburg heights, and that they could have been speedily carried, and the corps have been well on the road to Chancellorsville long before daylight. He also is of opinion that Brooks's division could have forced its way beyond Salem Church, with proper support. But we also know how gallant an attempt Brooks made to do this very thing, and how hard he struggled before yielding to failure.

It is in no wise intended to begrudge Gen. Howe his opinion; but he has certainly arrived at some of his conclusions, from premises founded on errors of fact.

The testimony of Col. Johns, which follows Gen. Howe's before the Committee on the Conduct of the War, bears only the weight to which the report of the commander of a brigade is entitled, whose duties allowed him to have but a partial view of the general features of the march. Though his opinion agrees with Gen. Howe's, he, too, mistakes the hour of the urgent order; and it is difficult to see why he was summoned before the Committee, unless as a partisan.

" My object " (continues Hooker) " in ordering Gen. Sedgwick forward at the time named, was to relieve me from the position in which I found myself at Chancellorsville on the night of the 2d of May." This statement is not only characteristic of Hooker's illogical method, but disingenuous to the degree of mockery. For this position, it will be remembered, was a strongly intrenched line, held by eighty thousand men, well armed and equipped, having in their front less than half their number of Confederates. In view of Hooker's above-quoted opinion about rifle-pits; of the fact that in his testimony he says: " Throughout the Rebellion I have acted on the principle that if I had as large a force as the enemy, I had no apprehensions of the result of an encounter ; " of the fact that the enemy in his front had been cut in two, and would so remain if he only kept the salient, just seized by Sickles and Pleasonton, at the angle south-west of Fairview, well manned ; and of the fact that he had unused reserves greater in number than the entire force of the enemy, — is it not remarkable that, in Hooker's opinion, nothing short of a countermarch of three miles by the

Sixth Corps, the capture of formidable and sufficiently manned intrenchments, (the work of the Army of Northern Virginia during an entire half year,) and an advance of nearly twelve miles, — all of which was to be accomplished between eleven P.M. and daylight of a day in May, — could operate to "relieve him from the position in which he found himself on the night of the 2d of May "?

"I was of the opinion, that if a portion of the army advanced on Lee's rear, sooner than allow his troops to remain between me and Sedgwick, Lee would take the road Jackson had marched over on the morning of the 2d, and thus open for me a short road to Richmond, while the enemy, severed from his depot, would have to retire by way of Gordonsville." Well enough, but was Sedgwick's corps the only one to accomplish this? Where were Reynolds, and Meade, and Howard, forsooth?

There is no particular criticism by Hooker upon Sedgwick's authority to withdraw to the north side of the river, or upon the necessity for his so doing. And we have seen how hard-pressed and overmatched Sedgwick had really been, and that he only withdrew when good military reasons existed, and the latest-received despatch of his superior advised him to do so. But Hooker states that " my desire was to have Gen. Sedgwick retain a position on the south side of the river, in order that I might leave a sufficient force to hold the position I was in, and with the balance of my force re-cross the river, march down to Banks's Ford, and turn the enemy's position in my front by so doing. In this, too, I was thwarted, because the messenger who bore the despatch to Sedgwick to withdraw and cover Banks's Ford, reached Sedgwick before the one who bore the order countermanding the withdrawal."

Hooker had indicated to Sedgwick that he wished him to take and hold a position at Taylor's, the point where the Fredericksburg heights approach the river, above the town, and terminate. But as these heights were by that time held by Early, and there were no pontoon-bridges there, the proposal was one Sedgwick knew could not be seriously entertained, with two-thirds of Lee's whole army surrounding his one corps, though he did reconnoitre the ground in a vain effort to carry out his chief's suggestions.

But was it not simpler for Hooker, who had now only Jackson's corps in his front, — some eighteen thousand men to eighty thousand, — to move upon his enemy, "attack and destroy him," and himself fall upon Lee's rear, while Sedgwick kept him occupied at Banks's Ford? And Hooker had all Sunday afternoon and night, and all day Monday, to ponder and arrange for attempting this simplest of manœuvres.

It is hard to understand how the man, who could cut out such a gigantic piece of work for his lieutenant, as Hooker did for Sedgwick, could lack the enterprise to execute so trivial a tactical movement as the one indicated. From the stirring words, " Let your watchword be Fight, and let all your orders be Fight, *Fight*, Fight ! " of April 12, to the inertia and daze of the 4th of May, is indeed a bewildering step. And yet Hooker, to judge from his testimony, seems to have fully satisfied himself that he did all that was to be expected of an active and intelligent commander.

The impression that an attack should have been made, prevailed among many of his subordinates. Gen. Wadsworth thus testified before the Committee on the Conduct of the War: " *Question.* — Can you tell why it was not ordered to attack the enemy at the time Gen. Sickles with his Third Corps was driven back; or why it was not ordered to attack the next day, when you heard the sound of Gen. Sedgwick's engagement with the enemy? *Answer.* — I have no means of knowing; at the time we were ordered to re-cross the river, so far as I could judge of the temper and spirit of the officers and men of the army, they were ready to take the offensive. I do not know why we were withdrawn then; I think we should not have withdrawn. I think the enemy were whipped; although they had gained certain advantages, they were so severely handled that they were weaker than we were."

" *Question.* — Is it your opinion as a military man, that, if our army had been ordered to take the offensive vigorously, we would have gained a victory there? *Answer.* — I think we should have taken the offensive when the enemy attacked Gen. Sedgwick."

Again Hooker: "During the 3d and 4th, reconnoissances were made on the right," (i.e., at Chancellorsville,) "from one end of the line to the other, to feel the enemy's strength, and find a way and place to attack him successfully; but it was ascertained that it could only be made on him behind his defences, and with slender columns, which I believed he could destroy as fast as they could be thrown on to his works. Subsequent campaigns have only confirmed the opinion I then ascertained."

Now, Hooker, at the time of giving this testimony, (March 11, 1865), had had nearly two years in which to become familiar with the true state of facts. He must have known these facts from the reports of his subordinates, if not from the accounts of the action in the Southern press. He must have known that all day Monday, he had only Jackson's corps opposed to him. He must have known that these troops had time enough to erect none but very ordinary intrenchments. And yet he excuses himself from not attacking his opponents, when he outnumbered them four to one. Would not his testimony tell better for him, if he had said that *at the time* he supposed he had more than eighteen thousand men before him? It is a thankless task to pursue criticism upon such capricious and revocatory evidence.

Sickles also, in his testimony, states that from our new lines we felt the enemy everywhere in his front, and that Gen. Griffin with his entire division made a reconnoissance, and developed the enemy in great force on our right flank. This work of reconnoitring can scarcely have been done with great thoroughness, for we know to a certainty what force Lee left behind. It would be well to say little about it. But it is not strange that the purposelessness of the commander should result in half-hearted work by the subordinates.

The following extract from the evidence of Gen. Sedg-wick before the Committee on the Conduct of the War,

compared with Hooker's and the actual facts, shows pal-
pably who is in the right.

"At nine A.M., May 4, I sent this despatch to Gen.
Hooker: 'I am occupying the same position as last night.
I have secured my communication with Banks's Ford.
The enemy are in possession of the heights of Fredericksburg in force. They appear strongly in our front, and
are making efforts to drive us back. My strength yesterday, A.M., was twenty-two thousand men: I do not know
my losses, but they were large, probably five thousand
men. I can't use the cavalry. It depends upon the condition and position of your force whether I can sustain
myself here. Howe reports the enemy advancing from
Fredericksburg.'

"*Question.*—When you were in the position on the 4th,
to which you have referred, were you where you could
have co-operated with the army at Chancellorsville in an
attack upon the enemy?

"*Answer.*—I could not proceed in that direction. I
think Gen. Hooker might have probably relieved me if
he had made an attack at that time. I think I had a
much larger force of the enemy around me than Gen.
Hooker had in front of him. There were two divisions
of the enemy on the heights of Fredericksburg, which
was in my rear; and they would have attacked me the
moment I undertook to proceed towards Chancellorsville.
About one A.M. of May 5, Gen. Hooker telegraphed me to
cross the river, and take up the bridges. This is the despatch: 'Despatch this moment received. Withdraw;
cover the river, and prevent any force crossing. Acknowledge receipt.'

" This was immediately done : as the last of the column was crossing, between three and four o'clock, the
orders to cross were countermanded, and I was directed
to hold a position on the south bank. The despatch was
dated 1.20 A.M., and was received at 3.20, as follows : —

" ' Yours received, saying you could hold position.
Order to withdraw countermanded. Acknowledge both.'

" In explanation of this I should say that I had telegraphed to Gen. Hooker that I could hold the position.
He received it after he had ordered me to cross over.
But, receiving his despatch to cross, I had commenced the
movement; and, as I have said, I had very nearly taken
my force over, when the order to cross was countermanded. To return at that time was wholly impracticable, and I telegraphed that fact to Gen. Hooker."

To place in juxtaposition Hooker's testimony and Sedgwick's, in no wise militates against the latter.

There is one broad criticism which may fairly be passed
upon Sedgwick's withdrawal across the Rappahannock.
It is that, with the knowledge that his remaining in position might be of some assistance to his chief, instead of
exhibiting a perhaps undue anxiety to place himself beyond danger, he could with his nineteen thousand men, by
dint of stubborn fighting, have held the intrenchments at
Banks's Ford, against even Lee with his twenty-four thousand.

But if he attempted this course, and was beaten, Lee
could have destroyed his corps. And this risk he was
bound to weigh, as he did, with the advantages Hooker
could probably derive from his holding on. Moreover, to

demand thus much of Sedgwick, is to hold him to a defence, which, in this campaign, no other officer of the Army of the Potomac was able to make.

Not but what, under equally pressing conditions, other generals have, or himself, if he had not received instructions to withdraw, might have, accomplished so much. But if we assume, that having an eye to the numbers and losses of his corps, and to his instructions, as well as to the character and strength of the enemy opposed to him, Sedgwick was bound to dispute further the possession of Banks's Ford, in order to lend a questionable aid to Hooker, how lamentable will appear by comparison the conduct of the other corps of the Army of the Potomac, under the general commanding, bottled up behind their defences at Chancellorsville!

XXXIII.

HOOKER'S FURTHER PLANS.

HOOKER states: "Gen. Warren represented to me that Gen. Sedgwick had said he could do no more; then it was I wanted him to take some position, and hold it, that I might turn the enemy in my immediate front. I proposed to leave troops enough where I was, to occupy the enemy there, and throw the rest of my force down the river, and re-enforce Sedgwick; then the whole of Lee's army, except that which had been left in front of Sedgwick, would be thrown off the road to Richmond, and my army would be on it.

"As soon as I heard that Gen. Sedgwick had re-crossed the river, seeing no object in maintaining my position where I was, and believing it would be more to my advantage to hazard an engagement with the enemy at Franklin's Crossing, where I had elbow-room, than where I was, the army on the right was directed to re-cross the river, and did so on the night between the 5th and 6th of May."

Now, the Franklin's Crossing plan, or its equivalent, had been tried by Burnside, in December, with a loss of twelve thousand men; and it had been fully canvassed and condemned as impracticable, before beginning the Chancellorsville manœuvre.   To resuscitate it can therefore serve no purpose but as an idle excuse.   And the argument of elbow-room, if made, is the one Hooker should have used against withdrawing from the open country he had reached, to the Wilderness, on Friday, May 1.

"Being resolved on re-crossing the river on the night between the 4th and 5th, I called the corps commanders together, not as a council of war, but to ascertain how they felt in regard to making what I considered a desperate move against the enemy in our front."   Be it remembered that the "desperate move" was one of eighty thousand men, with twenty thousand more (Sedgwick) close at hand as a reserve, against at the outside forty-five thousand men, if Early should be ordered up to re-enforce Lee.   And Hooker *knew* the force of Lee, or had as good authority for knowing it as he had for most of the facts he assumed, in condemning Sedgwick.   Moreover, from the statements of prisoners we had taken, very nearly an exact estimate could be made of the then numbers of the Army of Northern Virginia.

All the corps commanders were present at this conference, except Slocum, who afterwards came in.   All were in favor of an advance, except Sickles; while Couch wavered, fearing that no advance could be made to advantage under Hooker.   Hancock, (testimony before the Committee on the Conduct of the War,) says: "I understood from him" (Couch) "always that he was in favor of fighting then."   Hooker claims Couch to have been for retreat; but the testimony of the generals present, as far as available, goes to show the council to have been substantially as will now be narrated.

Hooker retired for a while, to allow free expression of opinion; and, with one exception, all present manifested a desire for another attack, in full force, — Howard, Meade, and Reynolds being especially urgent to this purpose. The one dissentient voice was Sickles; and he expressed himself, confessedly, more from a political than a strategic standpoint. He allowed the military reasons to be sound for an advance, and modestly refrained from putting his opinion against that of men trained to the profession of arms; though all allowed his right to a valid judgment. But he claimed, with some reason, that the political horizon was dark; that success by the Army of the Potomac was secondary to the avoidance of disaster. If, he alleged, this army should be destroyed, it would be the last one the country would raise. Washington might be captured; and the effect of this loss upon the country, and upon Europe, was to be greatly dreaded. The enemies of the administration were strong, and daily gaining ground. It was necessary that the Army of the Potomac should not run the risk of destruction. It was the last hold of the Republican party in Virginia. Better re-cross and recuperate, and then attempt another campaign, than run any serious risk now. These grounds largely influenced him in agreeing with the general-in-chief's determination to retire across the river. But there were other reasons, which Sickles states in his testimony. The rations with which the men had started had given out, and there had been no considerable issue since. Singularly enough, too, (for Hooker was, as a rule, unusually careful in such matters,) there had been no provision made for supplying the troops against a possible advance; and yet, from Sunday noon till Tuesday night, we had lain still behind our in-trenchments, with communications open, and with all facil-ities at hand to prepare for a ten-days' absence from our base. This circumstance wears the look of almost a pre-determination to accept defeat.

Now, at the last moment, difficulties began to arise in bringing over supplies. The river had rapidly risen from the effects of the storm. Parts of the bridges had been carried away by the torrent. The ends of the others were under water, and their entire structure was liable at any moment to give way. It was not certain that Lee, fully aware of these circumstances, would, for the moment, accept battle, as he might judge it better to lure the Army of the Potomac away from the possibility of vict-ualling. Perhaps Sedgwick would be unable to cross again so as to join the right wing. The Eleventh Corps might not be in condition to count on for heavy service. The Richmond papers, received almost daily through channels more or less irregular, showed that communications were still open, and that the operations of the Cavalry Corps had not succeeded in interrupting them in any serious manner. On the coming Sunday, the time of service of thirty-eight regiments was up. Many of these conditions could have been eliminated from the problem, if measures had been seasonably taken; but they now became critical elements in the decision to be made. And Hooker, despite his well-earned reputation as a fighting man, was unable to arrive at any other than the conclusion which Falstaff so cautiously enunciated, from beneath his shield, at the battle of Shrewsbury, that "the better part of valor is discretion."

XXXIV.

THE ARMY OF THE POTOMAC RE-CROSSES.

ORDERS were accordingly issued with a view to re-crossing the river; and during the 5th, Gen. Warren and Capt. Comstock of the engineers prepared a new and shorter line, in the rear of the one then held by the army, to secure it against any attempt by the enemy to interrupt the retreat. Capt. Comstock supervised the labor on the west side, and Gen. Warren on the east, of the United-States Ford road. "A continuous cover and abattis was constructed from the Rappahannock at Scott's Dam, around to the mouth of Hunting Run on the Rapidan. The roads were put in good order, and a third bridge laid. A heavy rain set in about 4.30 P.M., and lasted till late at night. The movement to re-cross was begun by the artillery, as per order, at 7.30 P.M., and was suddenly interrupted by a rise in the river so great as to submerge the banks at the ends of the bridges on the north bank, and the velocity of the current threatened to sweep them away." "The upper bridge was speedily taken up, and used to piece out the ends of the other two, and the passage was again made practicable. Considerable delays, however, resulted from this cause." "No troops took up position in the new line except the rearguard, composed of the Fifth Corps, under Gen. Meade, which was done about daylight on the 6th." " The proper dispositions were made for holding this line till all but the rearguard was past the river; and then it quietly withdrew, no enemy pursuing." (*Warren.*) The last of the army re-crossed about eight A.M., May 6.

Testimony of Gen. Henry J. Hunt: —

" A storm arose soon after. Just before sunset, the general and his staff re-crossed the river to the north side. I separated from him in order to see to the destruction of some works of the enemy on the south side of the river, which perfectly commanded our bridges. Whilst I was looking after them, in the darkness, to see that they had been destroyed as directed, an engineer officer reported to me that our bridges had been carried away, or were being carried away, by the flood. I found the chief engineer, Capt. Comstock; and we proceeded together to examine the bridges, and we found that they were all utterly impassable. I then proceeded to Gen. Meade's camp, and reported the condition of affairs to him. All communication with Gen. Hooker being cut off, Gen. Meade called the corps commanders together; and, as the result of that conference, I believe, by order of Gen. Couch at any rate, I was directed to stop the movement of the artillery, which was withdrawn from the lines, and let them resume their 'positions, thus suspending the crossing. On my return to the bridges, I found that one had been re-established, and the batteries that were down there had commenced re-crossing the river. I then sought Gen.

Hooker up, on the north side of the river, and proposed to him to postpone the movement for one day, as it was certain we could not all cross over in a night. I stated to him that I doubted whether we could more than get the artillery, which was ordered to cross first, over before daylight : he refused to postpone the movement, and it proceeded. No opposition was made by the enemy, nor was the movement disturbed, except by the attempt to place batteries on the points from which our bridges could be reached, and to command which I had already posted the necessary batteries on my own responsibility. A cannonade ensued, and they were driven off with loss, and one of their caissons exploded : we lost three or four men killed, and a few horses, in this affair. That is about all that I remember."

Gen. Barnes's brigade assisted in taking up the bridges; and all were safely withdrawn by four P.M. on Wednesday, under superintendence of Major Spaulding of the engineer brigade.

All who participated in this retreat will remember the precarious position of the masses of troops, huddled together at the bridge-heads as in a *cul-de-sac*, during this eventful night, and the long-drawn breath of relief as the hours after dawn passed, and no further disposition to attack was manifested by Lee. This general was doubtless profoundly grateful that the Army of the Potomac should retire across the Rappahannock, and leave his troops to the hard-earned rest they needed so much more than ourselves; but little thanks are due to Hooker, who was, it seems, on the north side of the river during these critical moments, that the casualties of the campaign were not doubled by a final assault on the part of Lee, while we lay in this perilous situation, and the unmolested retreat turned into another passage of the Beresina. Providentially, the artillery of the Army of Northern Virginia had expended almost its last round of ammunition previous to this time.

But several hospitals of wounded, in care of a number of medical officers and stewards, were left behind, to be removed a few days later under a flag of truce.

The respective losses of the two armies are thus officially given : —

FEDERAL LOSS.

General Headquarters and Engineers	9
First Corps	299
Second Corps	1,923
Third Corps	4,119
Fifth Corps	700
Sixth Corps	4,610
Eleventh Corps	2,412
Twelfth Corps	2,822
Pleasonton's Brigade	202
Cavalry Corps under Stoneman	189
	17,285

CONFEDERATE LOSS.

Jackson's Corps, —	
Early's division	851
A. P. Hill's division	2,583
Trimble's (Colston) division	1,868
D. H. Hill's (Rodes) division	2,178

Longstreet's Corps, —

Anderson's division	. . . . . .	1,180
McLaws's division	. . . . . .	1,379
Artillery	. . . .	227
Cavalry	. . . .	11

	10,277
Prisoners	2,000
	12,277

Both armies now returned to their ancient encampments, elation as general on one side as disappointment was profound upon the other.

Hooker says in his testimony before the Committee on the Conduct of the War: " I lost under those operations " (viz., the Chancellorsville campaign) "one piece artillery, I think five or six wagons, and one ambulance. Of course, many of the Eleventh Corps lost their arms and knapsacks."

The Confederates, however, claim to have captured nineteen thousand five hundred stand of small arms, seventeen colors, and much ammunition. And, while acknowledging a loss of eight guns, it is asserted by them that they captured thirteen.

The orders issued to the Army of the Potomac and the Army of Northern Virginia by their respective commanders, on the return of the forces to the shelter of their old camps, need no comment. They are characteristic to a degree.

HEADQUARTERS ARMY OF THE POTOMAC,
May 6, 1863.

GENERAL ORDERS No. 49.

The major-general commanding tenders to this army his congratulations on the achievements of the last seven days.   If it has not accomplished all that was expected, the reasons are well known to the army.   It is sufficient to say that they were of a character not to be foreseen or prevented by human sagacity or resources.

In withdrawing from the south bank of the Rappahannock before delivering a general battle to our adversaries, the army has given renewed evidence of its confidence in itself, and its fidelity to the principles it represents.

By fighting at a disadvantage we would have been recreant to our trust, to ourselves, to our cause, and to our country. Profoundly loyal, and conscious of its strength, the Army of the Potomac will give or decline battle whenever its interests or honor may command it.

By the celerity and secrecy of our movements, our advance and passage of the river were undisputed; and, on our withdrawal, not a rebel dared to follow us.   The events of the last week may well cause the heart of every officer and soldier of the army to swell with pride.

We have added new laurels to our former renown.   We have made long marches, crossed rivers, surprised the enemy in his intrenchments; and whenever we have fought, we have inflicted heavier blows than those we have received.

We have taken from the enemy five thousand prisoners, and fifteen colors, captured seven pieces of artillery, and placed *hors du combat* eighteen thousand of our foe's chosen troops.

We have destroyed his depots filled with vast amounts of stores, damaged his communications, captured prisoners within the fortifications of his capital, and filled his country with fear and consternation.

We have no other regret than that caused by the loss of our brave companions; and in this we are consoled by the conviction that they have fallen in the holiest cause ever submitted **to** the arbitration of battle.

By command of Major-Gen. Hooker.

S. WILLIAMS,
Assistant Adjutant-General.

HEADQUARTERS ARMY OF NORTHERN VIRGINIA,
May 7, 1863.

With heartfelt gratification, the general commanding expresses to the army his sense of the heroic conduct displayed by officers and men during the arduous operations in which they have just been engaged.

Under trying vicissitudes of heat and storm, you attacked the enemy, strongly intrenched in the depths of a tangled wilderness, and again on the hills of Fredericksburg, fifteen miles distant, and, by the valor that has triumphed on so many fields, forced him once more to seek safety beyond the Rappahannock. While this glorious victory entitles you to the praise and gratitude of the nation, we are especially called upon to return our grateful thanks to the only Giver of victory, for the signal deliverance He has wrought.

It is therefore earnestly recommended that the troops unite, on Sunday next, in ascribing to the Lord of Hosts the glory due unto His name.

Let us not forget in our rejoicing the brave soldiers who have fallen in defence of their country; and, while we mourn their loss, let us resolve to emulate their noble example.

The army and the country alike lament the absence for a

time of one to whose bravery, energy, and skill they are so much indebted for success.

The following letter from the President of the Confederate States is communicated to the army as an expression of his appreciation of their success : —

" I have received your despatch, and reverently unite with you in giving praise to God for the success with which he has crowned our arms. In the name of the people, I offer my cordial thanks to yourself and the troops under your command, for this addition to the unprecedented series of great victories which our army has achieved. The universal rejoicing produced by this happy result will be mingled with a general regret for the good and the brave who are numbered among the killed and the wounded."

R. E. LEE, *General.*

The following is equally characteristic : —

HEADQUARTERS ARMY OF THE POTOMAC,
CAMP NEAR FALMOUTH, VA., May 13, 1863.

To his Excellency, President of the United States.

. . . .

Is it asking too much to inquire your opinion of my Order No. 49? If so, do not answer me.

Jackson is dead, and Lee beats McClellan in his untruthful bulletins.

Very respectfully, your obedient servant,

JOSEPH HOOKER,
Major-General Commanding.

XXXV.

OPERATIONS OF THE CAVALRY CORPS.

A S was briefly related in the early part of this work, Hooker issued orders to Gen. Stoneman, the commanding-officer of the Cavalry Corps of the Army of the Potomac, on the 12th of April, to move the succeeding day for the purpose of cutting the communications of the enemy. The order read as follows: —

HEADQUARTERS ARMY OF THE POTOMAC,
CAMP NEAR FALMOUTH, VA., April 12, 1863.

Commanding Officer, Cavalry Corps.

I am directed by the major-general commanding to inform you that you will march at seven o'clock A.M., on the 13th inst., with all your available force, except one brigade, for the purpose of turning the enemy's position on his left, and of throwing your command between him and Richmond, isolating him from his supplies, checking his retreat, and inflicting on him every possible injury which will tend to his discomfiture and defeat.

To accomplish this, the general suggests that you ascend the Rappahannock by the different routes, keeping well out of the view of the enemy, and throwing out well to the front and flank small parties to mask your movement, and to cut off all communication with the enemy, by the people in their interest living on this side of the river. To divert suspicion it may not be amiss to have word given out that you are in pursuit of Jones's guerillas, as they are operating extensively in the Shenandoah Valley, in the direction of Winchester. He further suggests that you select for your place of crossing the Rappahannock, some point to the west of the Alexandria and Orange Railroad, which can only be determined by the circumstances as they are found on the arrival of your advance.

In the vicinity of Culpeper, you will be likely to run against Fitz Hugh Lee's brigade of cavalry, consisting of about two thousand men, which it is expected you will be able to disperse and destroy without delay to your advance, or detriment to any considerable number of your command.

At Gordonsville, the enemy have a small provost-guard of infantry, which it is expected you will destroy, if it can be done without delaying your forward movement. From there it is expected that you will push forward to the Aquia and Richmond Railroad, somewhere in the vicinity of Saxton's Junction, destroying along your whole route the railroad-bridges, trains of cars, depots of provisions, lines of telegraphic communication, etc. The general directs that you go prepared with all the means necessary to accomplish this work effectually.

As the line of the railroad from Aquia to Richmond presents the shortest one for the enemy to retire on, it is most probable that he will avail himself of it, and the usually travelled highways on each side of it, for this purpose; in which event you will select the strongest positions, such as the banks of streams, commanding heights, etc., in order to check or prevent it; and, if unsuccessful, you will fall upon his flanks, attack his artillery and trains, and harass him until he is exhausted and out of supplies.

Moments of delay will be hours and days to the army in pursuit.

If the enemy should retire by Culpeper and Gordonsville, you will endeavor to hold your force in his front, and harass him day and night, on the march, and in camp, unceasingly. If you cannot cut off from his column large slices, the general desires that you will not fail to take small ones. Let your watchword be Fight, and let all your orders be Fight, *Fight*, FIGHT ; bearing in mind that time is as valuable to the general as the rebel carcasses. It is not in the power of the rebels to oppose you with more than five thousand sabres, and those badly mounted, and, after they leave Culpeper, without forage and rations. Keep them from Richmond, and sooner or later they must fall into our hands.

The general desires you to understand that he considers the primary object of your movement the cutting of the enemy's communication with Richmond by the Fredericksburg route, checking his retreat over those lines ; and he wishes to make every thing subservient to that object. He desires that you will keep yourself informed of the enemy's whereabouts, and attack him wherever you find him.

If, in your operations, an opportunity should present itself for you to detach a force to Charlottesville, which is almost unguarded, and destroy depots of supplies said to be there, or along the line of the Aquia Railroad, in the direction of Richmond, to destroy bridges, etc., or the crossings of the Pamunkey, in the direction of West Point, destroying the ferries, felling trees to prevent or check the crossing, they will all greatly contribute to our complete success.

You may rely upon the general's being in communication with you before your supplies are exhausted.

Let him hear from you as often as necessary and practicable.

A brigade of infantry will march to-morrow morning at eight o'clock for Kelly's Ford, with one battery, and a regiment to the United-States Ford and Banks's Ford, to threaten and hold those places.

It devolves upon you, general, to take the initiative in the forward movement of this grand army; and on you and your noble command must depend, in a great measure, the extent and brilliancy of our success. Bear in mind that celerity, audacity, and resolution are every thing in war, and especially is it the case with the command you have, and the enterprise on which you are about to embark.

Very respectfully, your obedient servant,

S. WILLIAMS,
Assistant Adjutant-General.

In pursuance of which order, the corps broke camp near Belle-Plain, and encamped on the evening of April 13, beyond Morrisville. On April 14, it moved down to the vicinity of the bridge at Rappahannock station, which, after a slight skirmish by Gregg, was taken possession of. Beverly Ford, some miles above, was also examined, and the north bank occupied. Preparations for an early move on the morning of the 14th were made. Gen. Buford, commanding the cavalry reserve, remained at Kelly's Ford during the 14th, in order to draw the attention of the Confederates to that point, and indulged in a little artillery skirmish.

During the night a heavy rain set in, and before morning the river was no longer fordable by the artillery and pack-trains.

As is well known, it takes no great rainfall to swell the Rappahannock and Rapidan rivers, and their tributaries, to the proportion of torrents. Nor are more than a few hours necessary to raise these rivers and runs, and even the dry ravines, to an impassable depth. Gregg mentions in his report that a small stream, which, on the 13th, could be crossed at one step, had swelled to such a flood, that when, on the 15th, a regiment was obliged to cross it, there were lost one man and two horses by drowning.

So that, after crossing one division, Stoneman found that it would probably be isolated on account of the impracticability of crossing the rest of the corps, and consequently ordered its immediate return. And this was accomplished none too soon, by swimming the horses.

On reporting all these facts to Hooker, Stoneman was ordered to go into camp, where he remained, along the Orange and Alexandria Railroad, until the 27th.

The following letter is of interest, in this connection, as showing how keen Mr. Lincoln's intuitions occasionally were.

EXECUTIVE MANSION,
WASHINGTON, D.C., April 15, 1863.

MAJOR-GEN. HOOKER:

It is now 10.15 P.M. An hour ago I received your letter of this morning, and a few moments later your despatch of this evening. The latter gives me considerable uneasiness. The rain and mud, of course, were to be calculated upon. Gen. S. is not moving rapidly enough to make the expedition come to anything. He has now been out three days, two of which were unusually fair weather, and all three without hinderance from the enemy, and yet he is not twenty-five miles from where he started. To reach his point he still has sixty to go, another river (the Rapidan) to cross; and will he be hindered by the enemy? By arithmetic, how many days will it take him to do it? I do not know that any better can be done, but I greatly fear it is another failure already. Write me often. I am very anxious.

Yours truly,

A. LINCOLN.

On the 28th, Stoneman received the following additional orders: —

HEADQUARTERS ARMY OF THE POTOMAC,
MORRISVILLE, VA., April 28, 1863.

Commanding Officer Cavalry Corps.

I am directed by the major-general commanding to inform you that the instructions communicated for your government on the 12th instant, are so far modified as to require you to cross the Rappahannock at such points as you may determine between Kelly's and Rappahannock Fords, and for a portion of your force to move in the direction of Raccoon Ford and Louisa Court House, while the remainder is engaged carrying into execution that part of your original instructions, which relates to the enemy's forces and positions on the line of the Alexandria and Orange Railroad, and the line itself; the operations of this column to be considered as masking the column which is directed to move, by forced marches, to strike and destroy the line of the Aquia and Richmond Railroad.

You are further directed to determine on some point for the columns to unite; and it is recommended that it be on the Pamunkey, or near that line, as you will then be in position with your full force to cut off the retreat of the enemy by his shortest line. In all other respects your instructions, as before referred to, will remain the same.

You will direct all your force to cross to-night, or, if that shall not be practicable, to be brought to the river, and have it all thrown over before eight o'clock to-morrow morning. If the fords should be too deep for your pack-animals and artillery, they will be crossed over the bridge at Kelly's Ford.

You will please furnish the officers in command of these two columns with a copy of this, and of your original instructions.

Very respectfully, your obedient servant,

WM. L. CANDLER,
Captain and Aide-de-Camp.

These two orders would appear to be specific enough. The first is not modified by the second to any great extent; and the primary object of both is unmistakably to interrupt, by a bold stroke, Lee's main communications with Richmond by the Fredericksburg and Richmond Railroad.

The point on which the two columns, spoken of in the order of April 28, were to unite, was suggested as somewhere on the Pamunkey; and the one column was to go at once about its work, while the other masked its march, and after joined it.

Under these orders, Stoneman proceeded to get the corps together, — the distance of many outlying pickets delaying him almost a day, — and finally crossed the Rappahannock by five P.M. of the 29th, a portion of his troops using Kelly's Ford, in connection with Slocum's column.

He then assembled his division and brigade commanders, spread his maps before them, and made them acquainted with his orders and plans.

Averell, with his own division, Davis's brigade of Pleasonton's division, and Tidball's battery, was instructed to push for Culpeper Court House; while Stoneman, with Gregg's division, Buford's reserve brigade, and Robertson's battery, moved on Stevensburg.

It was expected that Averell would reach Brandy Station the same night (29th), driving before him the enemy, who was in very small force in his front. And when Stoneman got well on his way, he despatched Capt. Drummond, with a squadron, from beyond Rocky Run, by cross-roads, to Brandy Station, to bring intelligence of Averell's movements. The latter had, however, not reached that place. And, learning later in the evening that he had leisurely gone into camp, close by the place where the forces had crossed, Stoneman sent him word that he must turn the enemy in his front over to him, while himself pushed on towards Richmond.

This order read as follows : —

HEADQUARTERS CAVALRY CORPS,
April 30, 1863.

BRIG.-GEN. AVERELL, *Commanding, etc.*

The major-general commanding directs me to say that we have been delayed by high water, etc., and that he desires you to push the enemy as vigorously as possible, keeping him fully occupied, and, if possible, drive him in the direction of Rapidan Station. He turns the enemy over to you.

Very respectfully, your obedient servant,

A. J. ALEXANDER,
Assistant Adjutant-General.

And Hooker justly claims that it was an entire misinterpretation of his instructions, which were to have Averell join Stoneman's column, so soon as he had masked the latter's movement towards the Aquia and Richmond Railroad.

On May 3, Averell, who had done nothing but skirmish for a couple of days with a force of about one-fifth his own, and had then retired to Ely's Ford, and gone into camp, was relieved, and Pleasonton placed in command of his division.

The pack-mules and lead-horses of Stoneman's column were left with the main army, till the expected junction should be made by its advance south of the Rappahannock. Stoneman had with him but five or six days' rations; but he relied upon Hooker's assurance that he would be up with him before these rations were exhausted. Every officer and man, the generals and their staffs setting the example, took with them only what they could carry on their horses. Nor, despite the cold drenching rain, which fell plentifully, were any camp-fires lighted the first few nights. Stoneman seems to have been abundantly ambitious of doing his work thoroughly, and issued stirring orders to his subordinates, calling upon them for every exertion which they were capable of making.

On reaching Raccoon Ford, over the Rapidan, Stoneman found it guarded by the Confederate cavalry. He therefore sent Buford to a point six miles below, where he was able to cross, and, marching up the south bank, to uncover Raccoon Ford. The main body was then put over.

Stoneman's column was in the saddle by two A.M. of the 31st. But it proved to be too foggy to push on: he had as yet no guides, and he was obliged to wait for daylight.

He then hurried Gregg on to Louisa Court House, which place was reached during the night of May 1, and details were speedily set to work tearing up the railroads. Buford was sent by way of the North Anna to the same point; and at ten A.M., May 2, the entire force was at Louisa.

From here a squadron was despatched towards Gordonsville, to ascertain the meaning of the movement of several trains of troops, which had passed up from Richmond in that direction the evening previous. Parties were also sent out to Tolersville and Frederickshall Stations, to destroy whatever material could be found there. Still another destroyed Carr's Bridge on the North Anna.

The balance of the force was set to work to break up the Virginia Central; and for a distance of eighteen miles the telegraph, stations, tanks, and cars were burned, and the rails torn up, and bent and twisted over bonfires.

The command then marched for Yanceyville, on the South Anna, and, arriving at Thompson's Cross-roads at ten P.M. of May 2, headquarters were established at this point.

Here Stoneman seems to have become entirely oblivious of his instructions, and to have substituted for them ideas originating in his own brain. He assembled his officers, and informed them that "we had dropped like a shell in that region of country, and he intended to burst it in every direction."

Instead, therefore, of pressing with his main force for some point on the Fredericksburg and Richmond Railroad, and destroying it thoroughly, as he was particularly instructed to do, that being the one great object to be achieved, he contented himself with sending Kilpatrick with the Second New-York Cavalry, and Davis with the Twelfth Illinois Cavalry, to operate, the former against the railroad-bridges over the Chickahominy, and the latter at Ashland and Atlee; and also despatched Wyndham, of the First New-Jersey Cavalry, to strike Columbia, and destroy the canal-aqueduct over the Rivanna river, and if possible make a dash at the railroad-bridge over the Appomattox; while two regiments under Gregg were to follow down the South Anna to destroy its bridges, followed by the Fifth United-States Cavalry to see that the destruction was complete.

These parties were directed to rally on Stoneman, who was thus left with five hundred men of Buford's reserve, or else to push through to Gloucester Point, or Yorktown, as circumstances should dictate.

In pursuance of these orders, Gregg's column, which, on May 2, had burned the depots at Orange Court House, on May 3, moved down the South Anna, as far as the bridge where the Fredericksburg Railroad crosses the stream, and attempted to destroy it; but finding it protected by some infantry, and a couple of guns, he seems to have decided not to attack this force, and fell back upon the reserve. On the 5th, he destroyed the bridge at Yanceyville.

Kilpatrick marched some distance by daylight on the

3d, kept himself hidden through the day, marched again at nightfall, and reached Hungary Station at daylight the 4th. Here he destroyed the depot, and several miles of road, passed the Virginia Central at Meadow's Bridge, which he likewise burned, with all cars and material he could find in the vicinity, and camped at night in the rear of Hanover.

On the 5th, he pushed into Gloucester Point, destroying on the way a train of fifty-six wagons, and some twenty thousand bushels of corn in depots. He captured thirty prisoners, but paroled them.

Capt. Merritt with the Second United-States Cavalry, demolished a number of bridges and fords on the South Anna, and reached Ashland Station; but was unable to destroy the bridge at this place, which was guarded by an infantry force with part of a battery.

Col. Davis, on May 3, also reached Ashland, burned the trestle south of the town, and tore up the telegraph-line. He captured and destroyed some wagon-trains, containing about a hundred wagons, fired the depot and some material at Hanover, and bivouacked seven miles from Richmond. He was, however, precluded by his orders from trying to enter the capital, though he seems to have had a good opportunity for so doing.

On May 4, at Tunstall, on the York and Richmond Railroad, he met some resistance from a force of Confederate infantry with a battery; but, retracing his steps, he turned up in due season at Gloucester Point.

Col. Wyndham moved on to Columbia, where he rendered useless a large amount of stores, a number of canal-boats, and several bridges over the James-River canal. For lack of blasting-materials he was unable to destroy the aqueduct over the Rivanna river. It was solid enough to have delayed him at least forty-eight hours. The bridge over the James river to Elk Island he burned, and damaged the locks and gates of the canal as far as possible. He returned to Thompson's Cross-roads the same day with W. H. Fitz Lee at his heels.

Capt. Harrison, with a part of Buford's reserves, had, on May 4, somewhat of a skirmish with the enemy at Fleming's Cross-roads; but without effect upon the movements of the command. And another squadron crossed sabres with the enemy at Shannon's.

Such prisoners as were captured by any of the parties, were paroled at the time. A considerable number captured by Stoneman were sent to Richmond in one party, with word that the Union cavalry was following close upon them.

To quote Stoneman's own reasons, the six days' rations with which he left camp, having now been consumed, (though it would seem that there had been ample opportunity to collect as much more as was necessary from the stores destroyed); Hooker not having come up as expected; vague rumors having reached him of the defeat of the Army of the Potomac; having accomplished, as he deemed, all that he was sent to do; Averell having been withdrawn, thus leaving Lee ready to attack him, — Stoneman sent Buford with six hundred and fifty picked men to the vicinity of Gordonsville, and a small party out the Bowling-Green road, and marched his main body to Orange Court House.

At noon of the 6th, he assembled his entire command at Orange Springs; thence marched to Raccoon Ford, and crossed on the 7th.

On the 8th, the command crossed the Rappahannock at Kelly's, having to swim about twenty yards.

Leaving Buford to guard the river from the railroad to Falmouth, he then returned to camp.

During the latter part of the time occupied by these movements, the roads had been in very bad order from the heavy rains of the 5th.

Hotchkiss and Allen say, with reference to this raid: "This failure is the more surprising from the fact that Gen. Lee had but two regiments of cavalry, those under W. H. Fitz Lee, to oppose to the large force under Stoneman, consisting of ten or eleven thousand men. The whole country in rear of the Confederate Army, up to the very fortifications of Richmond, was open to the invader. Nearly all the transportation of that army was collected at Guineas depot, eighteen miles from Chancellorsville, with little or no guard, and might have been destroyed by one-fourth of Stoneman's force."

And further: —

"Such was the condition of the railroads and the scarcity of supplies in the country, that the Confederate commander could never accumulate more than a few days' rations ahead at Fredericksburg. To have interrupted his communications for any length of time, would have imperilled his army, or forced him to retreat."

They also claim that this column seized all the property that could be of use, found in their line of march.

" The citizens were in many cases entirely stripped of the necessaries of life."

Stoneman certainly misconceived his orders. These were plainly enough to throw his main body in Lee's .ear, so as substantially to cut his communications by the Fredericksburg and Richmond Railroad. To accomplish this, he was to mask his movement by a body of troops, which should keep whatever Confederate cavalry there might be in the vicinity of Orange Court House and Gordonsville, busy, until his main column was beyond their reach, and then should rejoin him; and to select a rallying point on the Pamunkey, so as to be near the important scene of operations. Every thing was to be subordinate to cutting the Fredericksburg and Richmond Railroad.

If Stoneman had properly digested his orders, and had pushed night and day for any available point on the Fredericksburg and Richmond Railroad, he might have reached it by Sunday. A thorough destruction of Lee's line of supply and retreat, would no doubt have so decidedly affected his strength, actual and moral, as to have seriously changed the vigor of his operations against both Hooker and Sedgwick.

Stoneman barely had time, from the lateness of his date of starting, to accomplish great results before Hooker was substantially beaten; but it would appear that he could have materially contributed to lessen the disastrous nature of the defeat, if no more.

His movements were characterized by great weakness. He did not seem to understand, that safety as well as success depended upon moving with a body large enough to accomplish results. Instead of this, he sent, to perform the most important work, bodies so small as to be unable to destroy bridges, when guarded by a few companies of infantry and a couple of guns.

And the damage done appears to have all been repaired by the time the raiders got back to camp.

Hooker's criticism in this instance is quite just: "On the 4th, the cavalry column, under Gen. Stoneman, commenced its return. One party of it, under Gen. Kilpatrick, crossed the Aquia and Richmond Railroad; and the fact that on the 5th, the cars carried the rebel wounded and our prisoners over the road to Richmond, will show to what extent the enemy's communications had been interrupted. An examination of the instructions Gen. Stoneman received, in connection with the official report of his operations, fully sustains me in saying that no officer ever made a greater mistake in construing his orders, and no one ever accomplished less in so doing. The effect of throwing his body of cavalry in the rear of the enemy, and on his communications, at the time it was in his power to have done it, can readily be estimated. But instead, that important arm of the army became crippled to an extent which seriously embarrassed me in my subsequent operations. Soon after, Gen. Stoneman applied for and obtained a sick-leave; and I requested that it might be indefinitely extended to him. It is charitable to suppose that Gens. Stoneman and Averell did not read their orders, and determined to carry on operations in conformity with their own views and inclinations."

XXXVI.

HOOKER'S RÉSUMÉ OF THE CAMPAIGN.

NEARLY two years after this campaign, in his testimony before the Committee on the Conduct of the War, Hooker thus speaks about the general result of the movement: —

"I may say here, the battle of Chancellorsville has been associated with the battle of Fredericksburg, and has been called a disaster. My whole loss in the battle of Chancellorsville was a little over seventeen thousand."

"I said that Chancellorsville had been called a disaster. I lost under those operations, one piece artillery, I think five or six wagons, and one ambulance." "In my opinion, there is nothing to regret in regard to Chancellorsville, except to accomplish all I moved to accomplish. The troops lost no honor, except one corps, and we lost no more men than the enemy; but expectation was high, the army in splendid condition, and great results were expected from it. It was at a time, too, when the nation required a victory." "I would like to speak somewhat further of this matter of Chancellorsville. It has been the desire and aim of some of Gen. McClellan's admirers, and I do not know but of others, to circulate erroneous

impressions in regard to it.   When I returned from Chan·
cellorsville, I felt that I had fought no battle; in fact, I
had more men than I could use; and I fought no general
battle, for the reason that I could not get my men in position to do so; probably not more than three or three and
a half corps, on the right, were engaged in that fight."

And he repeats his understanding of his manœuvring
as follows: "My impression was, that Lee would have
been compelled to move out on the same road that Jackson had moved on, and pass over to my right.   I should
add in my testimony that before leaving Falmouth, to
make this move, I had a million and a half of rations on
board lighters, and had gunboats in readiness to tow them
up to points on the Pamunkey River, in order to replenish
my provisions, to enable me to reach Richmond before the
enemy could, in case I succeeded in throwing him off that
line of retreat.   When I gave the order to Gen. Sedgwick,
I expected that Lee would be whipped by manœuvre.   I
supposed that he would be compelled to march off on the
same line that Jackson had.   He would have been thrown
on the Culpeper and Gordonsville road, placing me fifty
or sixty miles nearer Richmond than himself."

Criticism upon such an eccentric summing-up of the
results of the campaign of Chancellorsville, is too unprof-
itable a task to reward the attempt.   But assuredly the
commander of the gallant Army of the Potomac stands
alone in his measure of the importance of the movement,
or of the disastrous nature of the defeat.

XXXVII.

SOME RESULTING CORRESPONDENCE.

HEADQUARTERS ARMY OF THE POTOMAC,
NEAR CHANCELLORSVILLE, VA., May 5, 1863.

To the Commanding Officer,

    Confederate Forces, Chancellorsville, Va.

I would most respectfully request the privilege of sending a burial-party on the field of Chancellorsville, to bury the dead, and care for the wounded officers and soldiers of my command.

Very respectfully, etc.,

JOSEPH HOOKER,
Major-General Commanding.

HEADQUARTERS ARMY OF NORTHERN VIRGINIA,
May 6, 1863.

MAJOR-GEN. J. HOOKER,

    Commanding Army of the Potomac.

General, — I have had the honor to receive your letter of yesterday, requesting permission to send a burial-party to attend to your dead and wounded on the battle-field of Chancellorsville. I regret that their position is such, being immediately within our lines, that the necessities of war forbid my compliance with your request, which, under other circumstances, it would give me pleasure to grant. I will accord to your dead and wounded the same attention which I bestow upon my own ; but, if there

255

is any thing which your medical director here requires which we cannot provide, he shall have my permission to receive from you such medical supplies as you may think proper to furnish. Consideration for your wounded prompts me to add, that, from what I learn, their comfort would be greatly promoted by additional medical attendance and medical supplies.

I have the honor to be,

Respectfully, your obedient servant,

R. E. LEE, *General.*

HEADQUARTERS ARMY OF THE POTOMAC,
May 6, 1863, 4.30 P.M.

HIS EXCELLENCY A. LINCOLN,

President of the United States.

Have this moment returned to camp. On my way received your telegrams of eleven A.M. and 12.30. The army had previously re-crossed the river, and was on its return to camp. As it had none of its trains of supplies with it, I deemed this advisable. Above, I saw no way of giving the enemy a general battle with the prospect of success which I desire. Not to exceed three corps, all told, of my troops have been engaged. For the whole to go in, there is a better place nearer at hand. Will write you at length to-night. Am glad to hear that a portion of the cavalry have at length turned up. One portion did nothing.

JOSEPH HOOKER, *Major-General.*

EXECUTIVE MANSION, WASHINGTON, D. C.,
May 7, 1863.

MAJOR-GEN. HOOKER.

My dear Sir, — The recent movement of your army is ended without effecting its object, except, perhaps, some important breakings of the enemy's communications. What next? If possible I would be very glad of another movement early enough to give us some benefit from the fact of the enemy's communication being broken; but neither for this reason or any other do I wish any thing done in desperation or rashness. An early movement would also help to supersede the bad moral effect of the recent one, which is said to be considerably injurious. Have you already in your mind a plan wholly or partially formed? If you have, prosecute it without interference from me. If you have not, please inform me, so that I, incompetent as I may be, can try and assist in the formation of some plan for the army.

Yours, as ever,

A. LINCOLN.

HEADQUARTERS ARMY OF THE POTOMAC,
CAMP NEAR FALMOUTH, VA., May 7, 1863.

His Excellency, President of the United States.

I have the honor to acknowledge your communication of this date, and in answer have to state that I do not deem it expedient to suspend operations on this line, from the reverse we have experienced in endeavoring to extricate the army from its present position. If in the first effort we failed, it was not for want of strength or conduct of the small number of troops actually engaged, but from a cause which could not be foreseen, and could not be provided against. After its occurrence the chances of success were so much lessened, that I felt another plan might be adopted in place of that we were engaged in, which would be more certain in its results. At all events, a failure would not involve a disaster, while in the other case it was certain to follow the absence of success. I may add that this consideration almost wholly determined me in ordering the army to return to its old camp. As to the best time for renewing our advance upon the enemy, I can only decide after an opportunity has been afforded to learn the feeling of the troops. They should not be discouraged or depressed, for it is no fault of theirs (if I may except one corps) that our last efforts were not crowned with glorious victory. I suppose details are not wanted of me at this time. I have decided in my own mind the plan to be adopted in our next effort, if it should be your wish to have one made. It has this to recommend it: it will be one in which the operations of all the corps, unless it be a part of the cavalry, will be within my personal supervision.

Very respectfully, etc.,

JOSEPH HOOKER,
Major-General Commanding.

HEADQUARTERS ARMY OF NORTHERN VIRGINIA,
May 7, 1863.

MAJOR-GEN. HOOKER,

    Commanding Army of the Potomac.

General, — The reasons that prevented me from complying with your request with reference to your wounded no longer existing, I have the honor to inform you that you can extend to them such attentions as they may require. All persons whom it may be necessary to send within my lines for this purpose will remain until the wounded are finally disposed of. The burial of your dead has already been provided for.

I have directed that those of your wounded who desire it, shall be paroled and transferred within your lines, should you be willing to receive them; those in the vicinity of Chancellorsville at the United-States Mine Ford, and those on the battlefield of Salem Church at Banks's Ford or Fredericksburg. As your wounded generally occupy the few houses in the vicinity of the late battle-field, the transportation of this army cannot be employed in conveying them to the river until my own wounded have been removed to a place of shelter. As soon as this can be accomplished, I will cause such of your wounded as may desire to be paroled, to be delivered at the points above indicated, upon being advised of your willingness to receive them. In the mean time they shall have such care as is given to my own.

I have the honor to enclose a copy of my letter of yesterday in case the original may not have reached you.

Very respectfully, your obedient servant,

R. E. LEE, *General.*

HEADQUARTERS ARMY OF THE POTOMAC,
CAMP NEAR FALMOUTH, VA., May 7, 1863, 8 P.M.

GEN. R. E. LEE,
Commanding Confederate Forces at Fredericksburg, Va.

I have the honor to acknowledge the receipt of your two communications of May 6 and 7 this moment. If agreeable to you, I would like to send medical supplies and attendance to my wounded, and, at such times as the state of the stream will permit, send ambulances for them *via* the fords designated in your communications, viz., United-States and Banks's Fords. I will, with your consent, send parties to those fords with supplies at an early hour to-morrow. The swollen state of the Rappahannock probably preventing the crossing of any vehicles with supplies, I shall have to depend upon you for transportation for them. I will receive the wounded at the points named as soon as it can be done. I will send an officer to Chancellorsville, with your consent, to arrange the details, which, judging from your letter, with the state of the river, cannot now be determined by correspondence. Upon an intimation from you as to any deficiency in your immediate necessities of medical supplies of your own, by reason of their use for my wounded or other causes, I shall with pleasure replace them. I would be obliged for approximate information concerning the number of wounded, that a sufficient amount of supplies may be forwarded. I would be under obligations for an early reply.

> Very respectfully, etc.,
>
> JOSEPH HOOKER,
> *Major-General Commanding.*

(Copy furnished medical director.)

> HEADQUARTERS ARMY OF THE POTOMAC,
> CAMP NEAR FALMOUTH, VA., May 9, 1863.

GEN. R. E. LEE,

> *Commanding Army of Northern Virginia.*

The relatives and friends of several of the officers of this army who fell in the recent battles, have visited my headquarters with the view, if possible, of proceeding to the battlefields to recover the bodies of those near to them. I therefore have the honor to ask whether any person will be permitted to visit the battle-fields for the purpose indicated, or whether any arrangement can be made for sending to the lines of this army the bodies of such of our fallen officers as may have friends here seeking for them.

> Very respectfully, etc.,
>
> JOSEPH HOOKER,
> *Major-General Commanding.*

> HEADQUARTERS ARMY OF NORTHERN VIRGINIA,
> May 10, 1863.

MAJOR-GEN. JOSEPH HOOKER,

> *Commanding United-States Forces on the Rappahannock.*

General, — In reply to your communication of the 9th inst., I have the honor to state that it will give me pleasure to afford every facility to relatives and friends of officers killed in the late battles, to recover their bodies ; but I have no means of identifying them, or of ascertaining the fields on which they fell. If you will have me informed, I will cause search to be made.

Very respectfully, your obedient servant,

R. E. LEE, *General.*

APPENDIX.

In February and March, 1886, there was delivered at the Lowell Institute, in Boston, a series of lectures upon the late civil war, by the following gentlemen : —

Feb. 16. Introduction. Gen. Charles Devens of Boston.

Feb. 19. Pope's Campaign. Col. Jed. Hotchkiss of Staunton, Va.

Feb. 23. Antietam. Gen. George H. Gordon of Boston.

Feb. 26. Chancellorsville. Col. Theodore A. Dodge, U. S. Army.

March 2. Stonewall Jackson. Col. W. Allan of McDonough, Md.

March 5. Gettysburg. Gen. Francis A. Walker of Boston.

March 9. The Northern Volunteer. Col. T. L. Livermore of Boston.

March 12. The Southern Volunteer. Major H. Kyd Douglas of Hagerstown, Md.

March 16. Chattanooga. Gen. William F. Smith of Wilmington, Del.

March 19. The Wilderness. John C. Ropes, Esq., of Boston.

March 23. Franklin and Nashville. Col. Henry Stone of Boston.

March 26. The Last Campaign. Col. Fred. C. Newhall of Philadelphia.

These lecturers were well equipped for their task. Earnest study of their respective subjects had been attested by numerous volumes published by them relating to the war. The desire to have the truth told was apparent in the presence of three Confederate officers among the number ; and the special feature of the course seemed to be, that not only was the truth spoken in the most unvarnished manner, but that it was listened to with marked approval by overflowing audiences.

Perhaps the most invidious subject fell to my lot. What I said was merely a summary of the foregoing pages. But one point in my lecture aroused the ire of some of Gen. Hooker's partisans, and was made the subject of attacks so bitter that virulence degenerated into puerility. The occasion of this rodomontade was a meeting of Third-Corps veterans, and its outcome was a series of resolutions aimed at the person who had dared to reflect on Gen. Hooker's capacity, and to refer to the question of Gen. Hooker's habitual use of stimulants. The public mention of my name was as sedulously avoided as a reference to his satanic majesty is wont to be in the society of the superstitious; but the exuberance of the attack must have afforded unbounded satisfaction to its authors, as it very apparently did to the audience.

Following are the resolutions, which are of mild flavor compared to their accompanying seasoning of speeches: —

RESOLUTIONS.

The veterans of the Third Army Corps assembled here to-day, soldiers who served under Gen. Joseph Hooker in his division, corps, and army, re-affirm their lifelong affection for their old commander, their admiration for his brilliant achievements as one of the prominent generals of our armies, and protest against the recent revival of unjust assaults made on his conduct at Chancellorsville. Whether, after *one of the most noted tactical victories of modern times,* having placed the Army of the Potomac across the Rappahannock River on the flank of Lee, he might have gained a still farther advanced position; whether the failure of the cavalry to fully accomplish what was expected of it; whether the disaster to the Eleventh Corps and the delay in the advance of the Sixth Corps, — are to be attributed to errors of judgment of Gen. Hooker or of the subordinate commanders, are points which will be discussed again and again with profit to the military student. But we, who witnessed his successful generalship at Williamsburg, Glendale, Malvern Hill, Second Bull Run, and Antietam, have no language at our command strong enough to express our contempt for any one who, twenty years after the war, affirms that on any occasion in battle, with the lives of his men and the cause of his country in his keeping, Gen. Hooker was incapacitated for performing his whole duty as an officer by either the use of liquor or by the want of it.

We protest against oft-repeated statements that "Fighting Joe Hooker," while one of the bravest and ablest division commanders in the army, was possibly equal to handling a corps, but proved a failure as an independent commander. Assigned to the Army of the Potomac in January, 1863, after the disaster at Fredericksburg and the failure of oft-repeated campaigns, our army demoralized by defeat, desertions, and dissensions, Gen. Hooker re-organized his forces, stopped desertions, brought back to their colors thousands of absentees, and in three months revived confidence, re-established discipline, and enabled his army to take the field unsurpassed in loyalty, courage, and efficiency, as was shown at Chancellorsville and Gettysburg. We say Chancellorsville because, although not a victory for us, the campaign *inflicted on the enemy losses at least equal to our own;* and we say also Gettysburg because that victory was won by the army Hooker had re-organized, and led with such matchless skill from Falmouth to the eve of the battle.

Whatever ambition he may have had to command armies, it did not prevent his cheerfully serving his country under junior officers, giving them faithful support, and his record shows no instance of his removal from command by his superiors.

Here in his native State, amid the homes of so many of his old brigade, the survivors of the Third Army Corps, all witnesses of his genius, valor, and devotion to duty, indorse his record as a soldier, as a gentleman, and as a patriot, and sincerely believe that history will assign to Major-Gen. Joseph Hooker a place among the greatest commanders of the late civil war.

The italics are mine. "One of the most noted tactical victories of modern times," applied to Chancellorsville, is refreshing. Equally so is the exultant claim that "we inflicted on the enemy losses at least equal to our own." The infliction of loss on the enemy has always been understood by military men to be an incident rather than the object of war.

The following reply in "The Boston Herald" of April 11, 1886, explains itself: —

To the Editor of the Herald.

In the call for the meeting of the Third Corps Gettysburg Re-union Association, held at Music Hall on Fast Day, was the following clause: —

"Loyalty to the memory of our beloved commander, Major-Gen Joseph Hooker, makes it a duty, on this occasion, to protest against unjust and uncalled-for criticisms on his military record as commander of the Army of the Potomac."

It having been intimated to me by some old brother officers of the Third Corps, that my late Lowell lecture on Chancellorsville was the occasion of this proposed protest, I wrote to the chairman of the committee which called the meeting, asking for an opportunity to reply to this protest, within such bounds as even-handedness and the purposes of the meeting would allow. The committee answered that it could not see the propriety of turning the occasion into a public debate, and referred me to the press. I do not object to their decision, made, no doubt, upon what appeared to them sufficient grounds; but as the occasion was turned into a public debate — one-sided, to be sure — I ask you for space, to reply in your valued columns.

As an old Third-Corps man, I attended the meeting at Music Hall. The treasurer did not object to selling me a ticket to the dinner. I expected to hear some new facts about Hooker and Chancellorsville. I expected to hear some new deductions from old facts. I do not consider myself beyond making an occasional lapse even in a carefully prepared piece of work, and am always open to correction. But, to my surprise (with the exception of a conjecture that Lee's object in his march into Pennsylvania was to wreck the anthracite-coal industry), there was not one single fact or statement laid before the meeting, or the company at dinner, which has not already been, in its minutest details, canvassed and argued at a length covering hundreds of pages in the volumes on Chancellorsville, by Hotchkiss and Allen, Swinton, Bates, the Comte de Paris, Doubleday, and myself, not to speak of numberless and valuable brochures by others. The bulk of the time devoted to talking on this occasion was used in denunciation of the wretch — in other words, myself — who alleged that Joseph Hooker was drunk at Chancellorsville, or at any other time. This denunciation began with a devout curse in the chaplain's prayer, culminated in a set of fierce resolutions, and ended with the last after-dinner speech.

One thing particularly struck me. There was no one, of all who spoke, who began to say as many things in favor of Joseph Hooker as I for years have done; and not in fleeting words, but printed chapters. There was plenty of eulogy, in nine-tenths of which I joined with all my heart. But it was of the soldiers'-talk order, — cheering and honest and loyal, appealing to the sentiments rather than the intelligence. What I have said of Hooker has been solid praise of his soldierly worth, shown to be borne out by the facts. Barring, in all I say, the five fighting days at Chancellorsville, I have yet to find the man who has publicly, and in print, eulogized Hooker as I have done; and no one among the veterans gathered together Fast Day applauded with more sincerity than I, all the tributes to his memory. For though, as some one remarked, it is true that I " fought mit Sigel," and decamped from Chancellorsville with the Eleventh Corps ; it is also true that I passed through the fiery ordeal of the Seven Days, and fought my way across the railroad-cutting at Manassas, side by side with Joseph Hooker, under the gallant leadership of that other hero Philip Kearney.   It was very evident that but few of the speakers, as well as auditors, had themselves heard or read what I actually said.   The result of "coaching" for the occasion by some wire-puller was painfully apparent.   Let us see what was said.   I give the entire paragraph from my Lowell lecture : —

"It has been surmised that Hooker, during this campaign, was incapacitated by a habit of which, at times, he had been the victim.   There is, rather, evidence that he was prostrated by too much abstemiousness, when a reasonable use of stimulants might have kept his nervous system at its normal tension. It was certainly not the use of alcohol, during this time, which lay at the root of his indecision."

If that is an accusation that Hooker was then drunk, if it does not rather lean toward an exculpation from the charge of drunkenness, then I can neither write nor read the English language.   As is well known, the question of Hooker's sudden and unaccountable loss of power, during the fighting half of this campaign, coupled with the question of drunkenness, has been bandied to and fro for years.   The mention alone of Chancellorsville has been enough, ever since that day, to provoke a query on this very subject, among civilians and soldiers alike.   In a lecture on the subject, I deemed it judicious to lay this ghost as well as might be.   Had I believed that Hooker was intoxicated at Chancellorsville, I should not have been deterred by the fear of opposition from saying so.   Hooker's over-anxious friends have now turned into a public scandal what was generally understood as an exoneration, by intentionally distorting what was said into an implication that Hooker was so besotted as to be incapable of command. What I have written of his marching the army to this field and to the field of Gettysburg is a full answer to such unnecessary perversion. Let these would-be friends of Hooker remember that this calumny is of their own making, not mine. I am as sorry for it, as they ought to be. If the contempt expressed in the resolutions they passed had been silent, instead of boisterous, Hooker's memory would have suffered far less damage.

Gens. Sickles and Butterfield are doubtless good witnesses, though they sedulously refrained from any testimony on the subject, contenting themselves with declamation. But they are not the only good witnesses. After the loss of a leg at Gettysburg, I was ordered to duty in the War Department, where I served in charge of one or other bureau for seven years. I have heard this Hooker question discussed in all its bearings, in the office of the Secretary of War or Adjutant-General, by nearly every leading officer of the army, hundreds of whom had known Hooker from West Point up. I have had abundant opportunity of forming an opinion, and I have expressed it. Let him who garbles its meaning, bear the blame.

This action by many veterans of the Third Corps — even though procured by design from their thoughtless and open soldier's nature — is, however, much more sweeping and important. To the world at large it is a general condemnation of every thing which can be said in criticism of Hooker. It will reach far and wide, and in this light I desire to say what I do. The resolutions passed at the meeting explicitly protest against the statement that Hooker proved a failure as an independent

commander.   This needs notice at greater length than the question of sobriety or drunkenness.   Few have studied the details
of the campaign of Chancellorsville as carefully as I ; but
one other author has spread the facts so fully before the reading public.   No part of my recent criticism before the Lowell
Institute was new.   It was embodied at much greater length
four years ago, in my "History of Chancellorsville ; " the
reception of which volume by press, public, and soldiers, has
been its own best excuse.   Gen. Hooker, though making no
report, has put on record his explanation of this campaign.
Before the Committee on the Conduct of the War, he stated his
views as follows : " I may say here, the battle of Chancellorsville has been associated with the battle of Fredericksburg, and
has been called a disaster.   My whole loss in the battle of
Chancellorsville was a little over seventeen thousand. . . . In
my opinion, there is nothing to regret in regard to Chancellorsville, except to accomplish all I moved to accomplish.   The
troops lost no honor, except one corps, and we lost no more
men than the enemy ; but expectation was high, the army in
splendid condition, and greater results were expected from it.
When I returned from Chancellorsville, I felt that I had fought
no battle ; in fact, I had more men than I could use, and I
fought no general battle, for the reason that I could not get my
men in position to do so."

To speak thus of a passage of arms lasting a week and
costing seventeen thousand men is, to say the least, abnormal.

In trying to shift the onus of failure from his own shoulders
he said : " Some of our corps commanders, and also officers of
other rank, appear to be unwilling to go into a fight. . . . So
far as my experience extends, there are in all armies officers
more valiant after the fight than while it is pending, and when

a truthful history of the Rebellion shall be written, it will be found that the Army of the Potomac is not an exception."

This slur is cast upon men like Reynolds, Meade, Couch, Sedgwick, Slocum, Howard, Hancock, Humphreys, Sykes, Warren, Birney, Whipple, Wright, Griffin, and many others equally gallant. To call it ungenerous, is a mild phrase. It certainly does open the door to unsparing criticism. Hooker also concisely stated his military rule of action: " Throughout the Rebellion I have acted on the principle that if I had as large a force as the enemy, I had no apprehensions of the result of an encounter." And in his initial orders to Stoneman, in opening the campaign, came the true ring of the always gallant corps commander, " Let your watchword be ' Fight!' and let all your orders be, ' Fight, fight, fight!' "

I might here say that the only attempt, on Fast Day, to exculpate Hooker for the disaster of Chancellorsville was not of an order which can be answered. When one speaker asks, " If Gen. Hooker tells us that it was wise to withdraw across the river, is not that enough for you and me, my comrades?" I can only say that history is not so easily satisfied. To another speaker, who states that when Hooker had planted himself in Lee's flank by crossing the river, Lee ought, by all the rules of war, to have retreated, but when he didn't he upset all Hooker's calculations; that when Jackson made his " extra-hazardous " march around Hooker's flank, he ought, by all rules of war, to have been destroyed, but when he was not he upset all Hooker's calculations, and that therefore Hooker was forced to retreat, — it is quite beyond my ability to reply. When Gen. Sickles throws the blame upon Howard for the defeat of the Eleventh Corps, by reading the 9.30 A.M. order, without saying one word about Hooker's actions, change of plans, and despatches from that hour till the attack at 6 P.M., he makes any thinking man question seriously the sincerity of what he calls history.   When Gen. Butterfield indulges in innuendoes against Gen. Meade, whose chief of staff he was, and insults his memory in the effort to exculpate the Third Corps from a charge no one has ever made, or thought of making, against it, the fair-minded can only wonder why he goes out of his way to call any one to task for criticising Hooker.   Not one word was spoken on Fast Day which does not find its full and entire answer in the already published works on Chancellorsville.   It was all a mere re-hash, and poorly cooked at that.   To rely on the four reasons given by the Committee on the Conduct of the War as a purgation of Hooker from responsibility for our defeat at Chancellorsville, simply deserves no notice.   It is all of a piece with the discussion of the Third-Corps fight at Gettysburg on July 2.   No one ever doubted that the Third Corps fought, as they always did, like heroes that day.   What has been alleged is merely that Sickles did not occupy and protect Little Round Top, as he would have done if he had had the military *coup d'œil.*

Now, I desire to compare with Hooker's recorded words, and the utterances of Fast Day, the actual performance, and see what "loyalty to Hooker," as voted in Music Hall, means. Chancellorsville bristles with points of criticism, and there are some few points of possible disagreement.   Of the latter the principal ones upon which Hooker's formal apologists rely, are the destruction of the Eleventh Corps through Howard's alleged carelessness, and the failure of Sedgwick to perform the herculean task assigned to him in coming to Hooker's support. Allowing, for the moment, that Howard and Sedgwick were entirely at fault, and eliminating these two questions entirely from the issue, let us see what Hooker himself did, bearing in mind that he has officially acknowledged that he knew, substantially, the number of Lee's army, and bearing also in mind that the following are facts which can be disputed only by denying the truth and accuracy of all the reports, Federal and Confederate, taken as a body; and these happen to dovetail into each other in one so consistent whole, that they leave to the careful student none but entirely insignificant items open to doubt.

From Saturday at 8 A.M. till Sunday noon, some twenty-eight hours, Hooker with seventy-five thousand, and, after the arrival of the First Corps, nearly ninety thousand men, lay between the separated wings of Lee's army of twenty-four thousand and seventeen thousand men respectively, being all the while cognizant of the facts. Had ever a general a better chance to whip his enemy in detail? And yet we were badly beaten in this fight. Now, if loyalty to Hooker requires us to believe that his conduct of this campaign was even respectable, it follows that the Army of the Potomac, respectably led, could be defeated by the Army of Northern Virginia, two to one. Will the soldiers of the ever-faithful army accept this as an explanation of our defeat?

Again: from Sunday noon till Monday at 9 A.M., twenty-one hours, Hooker, with over eighty thousand men, was held in the White House lines by a force of twenty-seven thousand. If loyalty to Hooker requires us to believe that this was even respectable generalship, it follows that the Army of the Potomac, well led, could be defeated by the Army of Northern Virginia, three to one. Shall we accept this as an explanation of our defeat?

Again: from Monday at 9 A.M. till Tuesday at 4 P.M., thirty-one hours, against the advice of all his corps commanders except

Sickles and Couch (the latter agreeing to retreat only because he felt that the army would be defeated under Hooker whatever they might do), Hooker, with eighty thousand men, was held in the White House lines by a force of nineteen thousand, while the rest turned upon and demolished Sedgwick. If loyalty to Hooker requires us to believe that this was even respectable generalship, it follows that the Army of the Potomac, well led, could be defeated by the Army of Northern Virginia, four to one. Shall we accept this as an explanation of our defeat?

If there is in the world's military history a parallel to this extraordinary generalship, for which any one who has even pretended to study the art of war is able to find an excuse, I have failed to find such an instance in the course of many years' reading, and shall be happy to have it pointed out to me. Hooker's wound cannot be alleged in extenuation. If he was disabled, his duty was to turn the command over to Couch, the next in rank. If he did not do this, he was responsible for what followed. And he retained the command himself, only using Couch as his mouthpiece.

I have always maintained, that, man for man, the Army of the Potomac was at any time the equal of the Army of Northern Virginia, and that, man for man, the old Third Corps has proved itself good for Jackson's in its palmiest days. When, therefore, the Army of the Potomac was, as here, defeated or bottled up by one-half, one-third, or one-quarter its force of the enemy, my loyalty to that army demands that I seek a reason other than Hooker's alleged lack of heart of his subordinate officers. And this reason is only to be found in Hooker's inability to handle so many men. All the resolutions in the world, passed under a *furore* of misstatement and misconception, even by such a noble body of men as Third-Corps veterans, will not re-habilitate Joseph Hooker's military character during these five days, nor make him other than a morally and intellectually impotent man from May 1 to May 5, 1863. Loyalty to Hooker, so-called, is disloyalty to the grand old army, disloyalty to the seventeen thousand men who fell, disloyalty to every comrade who fought at Chancellorsville. I begrudge no man the desire to blanket facts and smother truth in order to turn a galling defeat into a respectable campaign ; I begrudge no man his acceptance of Hooker's theory that Chancellorsville was not a disaster ; I begrudge no one his faith in Hooker as a successful battle-field commander of the Army of the Potomac. But let it be well understood that this faith of necessity implies the fact that the Army of the Potomac was unable or unwilling to fight one-quarter its number of Lee's troops. I prefer my faith in the stanch, patient army, in its noble rank and file, in its gallant officers, from company to corps ; and I refuse to accept Hooker's insult to his subordinates as any explanation for allowing the Army of the Potomac to " be here defeated without ever being fought."

The Army of the Potomac was better than its commanders from first to last. It was, beyond speaking, superior to its commander during the fighting days at Chancellorsville. As a corps commander, Joseph Hooker will always be a type and household word. In logistics, even as commander of the Army of the Potomac, he deserves high praise. But when it comes to fighting the army at Chancellorsville, let whoso will keep his loyalty to Hooker, without protest from me. I claim for myself and the bulk of my comrades the right, equally without protest, sneers, or resolutions, to express my loyalty to the rank and file, my loyalty to the officers, and my loyalty to the army as a whole. And I claim, moreover, the right, without protest, sneers, or resolutions, to show that on this field it was the general commanding, and not the army, whose lapses caused defeat.   Not that I object to these Fast-Day resolutions.   I believe that I can still struggle onward in life, even under the contempt of their authors.   But partisanship in matters of history is a boomerang which always flies back to whack its thrower.   And Fast Day's performance was baldly partisan.

I am satisfied to abide the verdict of all soldiers, of all citizens, who ever studied the facts of this campaign.   Whatever the action of any meeting of old soldiers may be under partial knowledge of facts, under the influence of heated or sectional discussion, or under the whipping-in of a member of Hooker's staff, I do not believe that with the issue squarely put before them, and the facts plainly stated, any but a very inconsiderable fraction, and that not the most intelligent one, of the men of the Army of the Potomac, will give their suffrage to what has been suddenly discovered to be loyalty due to Gen. Joseph Hooker, as against loyalty to the Army of the Potomac.

The recent course of lectures at the Lowell Institute was intended to be a purely military one.   There was no intention of bringing politics or sectional pride into the discussion, and it was thought that the lectures could to-day be delivered without rousing a breath of ancient animosity.   If there was any campaign during our civil war which was especially, in a military sense, a glorious one for the rebels, and an ignominious one for us, it was Chancellorsville.   It is indeed a pity that the skill of the one side and the errors of the other cannot be once again pointed out, that the true and only possible explanation of Hooker's one hundred and thirty thousand men being defeated by Lee's sixty thousand cannot be once again stated, without eliciting from a body of veterans of the old Third Corps a set of condemnatory resolutions. There has been some very heated criticism of the recent lectures, and not a little fault-finding with the lecturers. I presume that none of the gentlemen who participated in the course would feel like denying the inference, so often suggested, that the censors might have done much better than they were able to do. Such censors generally can. These dozen lecturers have all been earnest students of our civil war, as is abundantly testified by the twenty odd volumes on the subject published by them since the reports of operations became available; and they keenly feel that modesty which is always bred of study. Such as they had, they were glad to give the public; nor do they in any wise shrink from generous disagreement or courteous criticism. I submit, however, that some of the carping which has been indulged in is scarcely apt to lead to the correction of errors, or the elucidation of truth. It is passing strange, that, at this late day, one may not criticise the military operations without arousing the evil spirit of the war. Can we not aim at truth, rather than self-gratulation, which will live no longer than we do? Criticism has always been indulged in, always will be. If a Frederick may be dissected by a Lloyd, if a Napoleon may be sat on in judgment by a Lanfrey, may not the merest tyro in the art of war be pardoned for reviewing Hooker? The gallant soldier who helped make history rarely writes history. The same spirit which sent him to the front in 1861 generally keeps him busy to-day with the material interests of the country. Despite the certainly novel fling of Fast Day at one who went into service as a mere boy, it remains a fact that rank, without the devoted study of years and a single eye to truth, will not enable any one to write history. It was proven beyond a peradventure on Fast Day, that the command of a corps, let alone a division, will not of itself breed a historian. Partisanship never will.

Truth will get written some day. I myself prefer to write as an American, forgetting North and South, and to pass down to those who will write better than any of us, as one who tried to speak the truth, whomsoever it struck. It is not I who criticise, who condemn Joseph Hooker: it is the maxims of every master, of every authority on the art of war. Not one of Hooker's apologists can turn to the history of a master's achievements, or to a volume of any accepted authority, without finding his pet commander condemned, in every action, and on every page, for the faults of the fighting days at Chancellorsville.

It was assumed on Fast Day that one should criticise only what he saw. I have never understood that Gibbon's "Decline and Fall of the Roman Empire" is any the less good because he did not live in the first few centuries of the Christian era, or that Jomini could write any less well of Frederick than of Napoleon. Service certainly helps a man in his researches or work, but it only helps. The best critic may be one who never served. I think I was the first officer to whom the Secretary of War permitted free use of the rebel archives for study. I have had good opportunities. How I have used them, I leave to others to say. It is easy to capture a meeting of honest-hearted veterans by such lamentable prestidigitation as was exhibited on Fast Day, and to pass any resolutions desired, by appealing to their enthusiasm. I prefer to be judged by the sober after-thought of men who are neither partisans, nor ready to warp facts or make partial statements to sustain their theories.

THEODORE A. DODGE.

Boston, April 10, 1886.